# The Altar Within

## A Radical Devotional Guide to Liberate the Divine Self

# Juliet Diaz

"Caring for myself is not self-indulgence,
it is self-preservation, and that is an act
of political warfare."

—Audre Lorde

Welcome to *The Altar Within*, an approach to Magic, spirituality, and healing like no other. *The Altar Within: A Radical Devotional Guide to Liberate the Divine Self* is a work of spiritual revolution for all peoples, offering them practices and rituals in the arts of self-worship, self-discovery, and self-activism.

Breaking through the vicious cycles of harmful and toxic spiritual practices and beliefs, this book is for those victimized and enslaved by colonization, offering a new take on personal development based in the resounding plea of our ancestors to live our Divined lives, the ones they could not have for themselves. *The Altar Within* brings the Magic to real life, acknowledging our humanness by connecting with our Spirit.

When we can finally decolonize our spiritual beliefs, Divinity can be a super force in our lives, making us whole, stronger, wiser, and setting us on a path of transcendent activism #magicalaf. In this life-changing work, you will be learning deep subconscious and mindset techniques to take your spiritual and magical practice to the next level, healing deep trauma and finally living your Divined life.

Please note the QR codes at the beginning and end of this book are a free offering of rituals, ceremonies, meditations, daily exercises, journaling, and resources to help and support you in this work. I hope you choose to use them as together we kneel before *The Altar Within*.

*Row House Publishing recognizes that the power of justice-centered storytelling isn't a phenomenon; it is essential for progress. We believe in equity and activism, and that books—and the culture around them—have the potential to transform the universal conversation around what it means to be human.*

**Some of the rituals and practices in this book include physical prompts for breathing, hand placement, reciting phrases, etc. Acknowledging that we all experience our physical bodies differently, the QR code bonus materials include modifications for each physical exercise. This book is for you; use it in whatever way serves you best.**

Library of Congress Cataloging-in-Publication Data Available Upon Request

ISBN number 978-1-955905-00-8 (HC)

ISBN number 978-1-955905-06-0 (eBook)

Printed in the United States

Distributed by Simon & Schuster

*Book design by Pauline Neuwirth, Neuwirth & Associates, Inc.*

*Illustrations by Annie Tarasova (@dreamy_moons)*

First edition

10 9 8 7 6 5 4 3 2 1

I am dedicating this book to my Divine Self.

For she dismantled and disrupted me until I found myself hidden beneath all

that did not belong to me or serve me. Because of her, I am whole, and because

I am whole, I can show up for myself and others.

# Contents

# Contents

# Introduction

"Breathe in and exhale. Breathe in and exhale."

"Come on," I told myself. "You've done this hundreds of times before. Breathe in and . . . ugh."

But something was wrong. "Why can't I keep my mind clear? What's happening?"

My thoughts started to run rampant, flooding my mind with ghosts hidden within bone. I was sitting in front of my mirror doing a meditative ritual, one I'd done many times before, one that helps me come back to self and detach from what no longer serves me. But, this time, it was different. I suddenly felt paralyzed, with no voice, no sight—just memories streaming before me. My life was flashing by, and all I could think was, Am I dying?

I could see myself at seven years old, standing on the edge of a seven-story building, ready to jump off; then my mind flashed to another time when I was eighteen and homeless, sitting in the corner of an abandoned monastery, starving, barely able to keep my head up. The next memory was when I was twenty-seven: My feet were bruised and cracked from pacing back and forth for hours in my kitchen, mascara dripping down my face and lipstick smeared across my mouth. This was the day I signed the divorce papers; I was now a single mother of two babies with absolutely no idea where I was going.

I wanted the memories to end. I thought that if I could make whatever this was stop, it would go away.

I pleaded, "Please. Stop!"

All of a sudden, a larger-than-life Wolf stood in front of me, her amber eyes glaring into my Spirit as she gently sent a message through my spine: "Let go."

Gasp.

Let go? Shivers cut into my flesh, the blade sharpened by so many years of anguish. Why was I so afraid to let go? Wasn't this what I'd wanted all along? Since childhood, I had worked to embody the spiritual being. I had spent countless hours meditating, performing rituals, journaling, and participating in Ceremony, declaring affirmations of my new self. I had committed to shadow work, inner-child work, self-love, and self-care. I'd worked hard to get to this moment, but suddenly, I feared the ghost of my liberation.

I had been trying to heal wounds that were deeper than the Grand Canyon. Shit, they were more like a cave. I didn't know what I was going to find in there, and I was terrified to enter. So often, I thought that if I could just throw some TNT in, I could explode the pain out of existence. But that's not how this works, is it? We'd just end up trapped inside. It felt like the more I worked on healing, the more broken I became.

And yet, deep inside, I knew there was nothing to fear. I knew that the ghosts that live within us are purely reflections of the things we have yet to forgive. Clearly, this was my wake-up call. And so, with the might of a thousand ancestors, I let go.

And I released a howl that permeated through my soul: "Aaaaooooooooo!"

Little did I know that on the other side, my husband was trying to wake me. He couldn't find a pulse; he couldn't feel my breath. He was sure I was dead. He called the hospital, but they told him not to come; they were overwhelmed with COVID cases. Instead, he held me in his arms, holding space for me and keeping faith that I would come back, whatever that meant.

I had been yanked from my body and thrust into the darkest of oceans, where time ceased to exist. I was lifeless yet witness to it all. I was slowly falling deeper into the abyss, my naked body in rest, just simply being. The humming of the sea mesmerized me as the light escaped, and my mind finally went silent.

Through the deafening silence, I heard an echo of a voice say, "Take your first breath."

Spirit, is that you? I asked. But before I could question anything else, I felt the breath of light fill my brokenness. For just a moment, I was held by my own soul, surrounded by an orchestra of bliss and truth coming to bring me out of the infinite night. The galaxies became still as I began to hear the delicate song of my soul's remembering.

I opened my mouth and took a deep breath in, swallowing that dark ocean into my being, and with a big gasp, *I woke up,*

I heard myself say, in an ancient tongue, "By ignoring the sacred responsibility of taking care of ourselves—body, mind, and Spirit—we disrespect sacredness and wholeness. Instead, we should be worshipping ourselves, discovering our limitless potential, and liberating the Divine within."

So, was that it? Was that what I'd been missing all these years in my spiritual practice? Was that what we'd all been missing? Was it the simple fact that looking outside ourselves for answers and guidance was actually slowly suffocating the Spirit within?

Because, think about it: How many self-help books have you purchased? Self-improvement audiobooks? How many personal development podcasts have you listened to or spiritual teachers have you followed? How much money have you spent on spiritual readers trying to form a connection to the feelings you already have within you? Now, there is nothing wrong with having spiritual guidance from these sources, but depending on them solely and neglecting the all-powerful Spirit you carry within keeps you from evolving, expanding, and embodying your ultimately limitless potential. I love having a spiritual team of people and Spirits I trust for assistance and motivation, but what I realized out there in that dark ocean was that they weren't the answer. I was—and I always had been—the liberation I sought.

What if I told you that you will need nothing but the *self* to heal, to discover your truth, to master your power, and to start building the life you have always desired? What if you finally believed that you were created with all the tools you need, flawless and sacred AF? What if you, too, went out there into that dark ocean of your deepest fears? What wisdom might you find?

And what wisdom might you bring back?

This book is the message I received upon waking. It is the wisdom of that dark space translated into practices. *The Altar Within* is like no other approach to spirituality; it may even be controversial to some. After all, worshipping something other than God is not the norm. Yet I now see the worship of the self as an even more powerful way of connecting with Spirit. It is not replacing your God; it is adding to your worship the most important link: *you.*

Since colonization and the rise of religions and gatekeepers and the brainwashing of hierarchy, people have feared the power that lives within them. They have been programmed to believe that real magic and power are unattainable, that they live outside of us and are only accessible to the "chosen ones." Heck, most believe that the concept of self-worship is downright evil and can only come from malicious entities. But when I woke up, I realized that I could no longer accept that my innate birthright could also be used as a weapon against me.

For so long, our spiritual practices have been rooted in #lightandlove and #goodvibesonly. And yet so many of us feel disconnected from these easy slogans meant to apply to dark oceans and impossibly Divine principles. I knew that the message I had received required the dismantling of who I wasn't and the remembering who I *am.* I knew that it was time to create a practice that would radically change the world of magic and spirituality as we know it, offering eye-opening shifts that could change and mold our lives in the most extraordinary ways.

*The Altar Within* is a devotional to self that will ultimately bring into focus the being you have always been. It offers a practice meant for us all, in this new world, in these revolutionary times, a practice where decisions aren't about you or anybody else—they are spiritual, connecting us back to the stillness of the galaxies, the Divine Self within.

Is this an awakening? Maybe. But awakening to something simply means remembering. You are already an enlightened being; however, the world tells us to seek—seek enlightenment, seek beauty, seek wholeness, seek sacredness—when we are already all those things. The misunderstanding lies in the belief that we must attain something, when in truth we must detach ourselves from the things that tell us we aren't whole.

# Introduction

We all go through life-changing shifts in our lifetimes; I use to call them mini awakenings. This last one wasn't so mini. In fact, it is still alive and expansive today. This work that I've been doing all these years was not a waste of time but a journey that got me to where I am right now, sitting here in my new home, on a mountain, writing this book. The only thing that shifted was perspective and where I placed my energy. Energy, after all, is sacred currency; our greatest task is to spend it wisely.

I left social media in December 2020, right after this experience, and did not plan to return until I felt called to. I mentally struggled with this new perspective and had to adjust and make room for this new practice, unlearning and liberating my soul. I saw life as we know it like a great big play where we all have roles—a matrix, as some call it.

I could not merge reality with this expansive being for months. I fasted, took a vow of silence, and even had a funeral for the parts of myself I had let go of. I continued my spiritual practice, but, from this new perspective, I began to find myself, my truth, and my power in ways I never thought were possible. All of me. Happy, whole, understanding, compassionate, passionate, forgiving, patient, and joyful. OMG, the joy. Even the healing felt blissful. I was now working with and feeling fully connected to my mind, body, and soul. It was as though I had been plugged back into divinity.

It has been eight months now, and I am unrecognizable to those who still have contact with me. I've healed at a level that I'd never been able to reach before; my mental state and body have transformed in such a short time. But am I completely healed? Ha, no—healing is a slow slither through your journey on this Earth—but the depths I've been able to reach have been life changing.

But as I have also learned, healing is a journey that is better when shared. We can never fully heal until all are healed. And so I bring you *The Altar Within*, a devotional guide that weaves together self-worship, self-discovery, and self-activism. It offers a practice that will uplevel your life, elevate your Spirit, and evolve your mind. And the main character is you! We are going to take away some harmful beliefs that have been engraved in our heads and implement a new way of self-love, manifestation, and community into our daily lives.

All I wish is for you to feel the bliss that can be found in each and every part of you. This bliss is a love that is intertwined with your creation—it's a gift from divinity and one that will get you through the most challenging times of your life. We don't need to become anything other than who we already are. And we don't need to look elsewhere for the pieces we already hold. We are not here to achieve perfection, alignment, or balance with a side of only good vibes. #fuckperfection #fuckgoodvibesonly

*The Altar Within* will guide you through a surrender so raw and powerful that, in the process, you will discover a Divine peace in your Spirit that is a direct love from the expansive universe you are made of. And that love will shift your focus and seeking into *you*, fully and unapologetically, without any need for outside sources of power; it will allow you to break through old habits and patterns, heal deeply, and reach your highest potential by building an intimate relationship with Spirit, all while seeing yourself from a different lens, understanding your truth, and truly falling in love with all of who you are.

So let's go, bestie! And yes, my wonderful Soul, we are already besties. We are doing the kind of work that requires friendship—trusting, deep, and magical.

This isn't a one-size blueprint that fits all; we all have our own unique architecture to discover, and you will discover it within yourself. If you are reading this book, it is meant for you. I do not believe in coincidences, and soon neither will you. Whether you are new to the magical, spiritual world or a veterana Spiritual Baddie, this is for you! Your Spirit is ready!

Your ancestors are screeeeeeeeeaaaaming and rooting for you!

Take a deep breath in, and exhale.

# A Note on Liberation

A s I mentioned, I am spiritual AF. I am a bruja and a seer from a long line of healers and brujas on both my parents' sides. I've been practicing since I was a child. Life hasn't always been good to me; in fact, I did not feel as if I was truly living until I reached my thirties. I am now forty. Even though I was always in survival mode, I still dreamed and believed I was meant for more than the cards I was handed. And yet, those lessons and trials I went through made me better able to see the light in even the darkest times. I took a good look at my life and saw so many things undone, piles of books unread, and my body unhealed and struggling, as I consistently prioritized productivity over rest. My energy was placed in so many things, but none of it was put toward the thing that mattered the most: my inner Altar.

"But you said you were spiritual AF," you might say. "If you did all that spiritual work, self-care, and self-love, how was your life so messy? Untouched? Complicated?"

Good question! I thought the same until the message of this awakening finally made sense to me. You see, spirituality as we know it isn't all flawed, but there is a misleading notion of embodiment, aligning, balance, perfection, and the mightily fucked-up belief that you should be vibrating high at all times and be positive on the daily to achieve enlightenment, awakening, or manifestation.

I used to do the things that we are all told to do when living a spiritual life: "Do the work" and "Stay positive." And so we do the work, day in and day out. We shut the noise out of our inner selves, screaming and brewing up storms within us. We buy all the crystals, light the incense and the candles, pray to gods and goddesses, ask and plead for better days, a better self, a better life. Or if you are into manifesting (which I am!), we push the negative thoughts out, ignore them, and pretend there aren't any dark creatures in our minds to bring our frequencies down because, God forbid, if we feel an ounce of anything that's not positive, we won't manifest what we desire.

That is some whitewashed, full-of-privilege way of practicing the Divine.

If this is how spirituality is supposed to be lived, then we immediately contradict the belief that we are one. We are leaving out those people who can't afford to buy all the tools, pay for expensive memberships, be in high spirits daily, practice the same way, or believe in the same things. We are leaving out people who have real-life issues to deal with, people who can't escape to an island to reset every month like we see these "spiritual leaders" do on social media. The message is toxic and violent, especially to BBIPOC and LGBTQ+ communities.

This false notion makes those with more challenging past wounds or even current issues feel less than. So these people end up feeling like they aren't meant for greatness, that they aren't worthy, or sacred, or important to the web we *all* weave in this existence. For most of us, healing is never-ending. There is a disconnect between the world the spiritual community paints and the world in which we live. #normalizereallife

I finally understood why I was struggling and why my practice was draining me and causing harm. Doing the work looks beautiful and peaceful to those who have the resources, or to people without illness, mental health issues, and who don't come from a past with trauma. But for people like me, doing the work can be downright agonizing, triggering, and ugly AF. Most days were good, but on many days, even getting out of bed was hard. I was striving for perfection, good vibes only, light and love, but all the while, the world we live in was falling apart: The people we love, our families, and our communities are suffering, dying, and facing injustices. Our Earth is sick and fleeting. I wasn't a spiritual being who ignored the real world and could escape into my little fantasy land. In fact, I didn't want to.

I knew that the Divine was bigger than some filtered picture on Instagram. The Divine was also the suffering, the dying; it was facing the injustice. I couldn't continue to be a leader in this community if disconnection from suffering was required for enlightenment. I started to question my wholeness and sacred duty on this Earth. And that disconnection started to show up in my body—inflammation, lupus, mental instability, mood swings, and tics in my neck. I was one hundred pounds overweight, and depression was getting the best of me. It got hard to focus, more challenging to create, and harder and harder to believe and have faith in Spirit.

Even with all the spiritual work I was doing and all the good things happening in my life—my book becoming a bestseller, my career as an author taking off, media covering me in features, money flowing in abundantly—I still felt a sense of falseness and unworthiness. I still felt disconnected. And so, Divinity stepped in and showed me a new way, a new perspective that works for those of us who want to achieve greatness and manifest our wildest dreams but who also struggle to keep a high vibe all the time. This book is for the witches in the moonlight, the dreamers in the shadows, and the lightworkers living among the chaos.

The goal isn't to have a positive mindset all the time; it is to be awakened to the self. This way, it's easier for us to understand how we're feeling and why we're feeling a certain way, checking ourselves on our own bullshit, adjusting and coming back home to self. When we become observers of our own lives, we can see the areas that need attention, love, and healing. We can create self-honesty and self-discipline.

Yes, we want to have more days of positivity, more good vibes sometimes, but we can't achieve that if we don't acknowledge our hardships, shadows, and inner ghosts. None of these things make us less spiritual; in fact, truth is the embodiment of the Divine.

In this new perspective, we avoid being reactive. We stop faking it until we make it. We begin to truly feel the spectrum of human emotion, to experience more of the positive mindset we all want to achieve. This isn't an easier way of practicing; in fact, it will be more complex work, but it is a way that allows us to be, just as we are, while we do the work without believing that some outside person, program, or philosophy is our shortcut to spiritual healing.

Your spiritual practice looks like however you want it to, not like anyone else's. The work needs to be done, but it's the shift in energy and perspective that will make the work so much more achievable, tolerable, and impactful. #progressnot-perfection

In this practice, you are sacred, honie! No matter your current situation, social status, mood, or vibration. You're a bad bitch, a Queen who puts self first, before anything or anyone else. Whether you are winning at life and feeling yourself or having a tough day, week, or month, you will learn how to worship the ground you walk on.

Connecting to the Altar within is a practice in reclaiming your power, magic, mind, body, and Spirit. It is a remembrance of who you truly are. It is you taking responsibility for your own life, health, growth, and expansion. No one else is going to do this for you; no one else is coming to save you or to magically manifest your life in the direction you want it to go. You are capable of taking your power back, of freeing yourself and creating a life you have always dreamed of.

We all know that most of us were stripped from these rights, and it is up to us to reclaim them, demand them back, demand a more just, sustainable, and equitable world for us all.

You can't just say, "I will reclaim," "I will unlearn," "I will decolonize"; these things all take real work to achieve. They require a sacred devotion to self. Honoring the Altar within creates a powerful spiritual practice that becomes a force for all, one that supports your unique needs and wants because you become the creator, caretaker, and protector of your inner and outer worlds. True magic is realizing you have an innate birthright to live in joy, be healthy, and live your Divined life. There is a deep and magical life flowing through you at all times; you just have to stay still enough to feel the direction of its current.

For many, we've forgotten our ability to feel wholeness and connectedness to our Divine selves, especially our connection to our communities, to Earth, and to all her children. Doing yoga, meditation, breathwork, spell work, and so on is not going to fix anything if there isn't a genuine intention, direction, and connection to those tools and practices. So we must learn to implement real intention in all that we do to create rituals that actually work to support ourselves.

Have you ever been devoted to something, so devoted that nothing could separate you from it? Well, this is what self-worship is, a devotion to self so powerful that not even you can sabotage it. Meaning, you will never give up on yourself again. You will always be working to connect into that Divine Self, following her guidance by going inside yourself so deeply that nothing can distort your own truths.

Through your Altar within, you can get to know yourself in a way no one else has ever known you and you have never known anyone else.

In self-worship, you learn to become the ritual in the Ceremony that is life—taking your power back and reclaiming your joy, liberation, and truth. It is a practice of commitment to take better care of yourself, to mindfully heal and radically accept yourself, but in doing so, you begin to take responsibility for your life, learn to treat yourself better, and build compassion as you overcome your inner critic (while also learning the importance of self-activism in the form of community care).

Self-discovery is becoming authentic, from your roots to your Spirit. When we discover our true selves, there is a lot we must release in order to allow for our light to shine through. We take self-love very seriously, overcoming roadblocks that make it hard for us to love ourselves and creating a solid support system within ourselves and in our lives. We work through the importance of self-patience, tuning in to the timing of the Divine. And we practice the art of self-forgiveness, letting go of what does not serve us anymore and facing the truths that continue to haunt us. We strip away all of it until we feel fully present in our magic.

Self-activism is combining all of this together and putting it into practice. The more we practice, the more we learn to master the self. This is especially important when preventing outside forces from interfering with our sacred journey and purpose on this Earth. Spirituality and wellness spaces have been overrun by whiteness, mimicking racist belief systems that keep us all collectively oppressed. When people in these spaces weigh in on what we "need" or must attain, or when they tell us what our liberation, bodies, or spiritual practices should look like, they make us believe that we need them for our own healing and ascension.

By self-worshipping, discovering, and liberating the Divine Self, we are dismantling these systems from within. By devoting yourself to a practice that requires you to connect to your truth and Divine Self, the very place where these beliefs have been embedded, you will start to realize that the capitalist, colonialist parts of spirituality are not here to heal us but rather to destroy our relationship with our inner selves. These practices have ingeniously created a simple yet intrusively harmful system that keeps us from seeing ourselves as we truly are: powerful, self-healing, whole, Divinely guided, connected, and capable of manifesting anything we believe in.

Instead, modern wellness has worked to distort our truths, profiting from our need for healing while appropriating spiritual and Indigenous cultures, medicine, and wisdom. The wellness industry includes some of the biggest and most successful businesses—and yes, wellness is a business. Yet it only works in favor of white privileged people because it was built that way. The thing is, instead of wasting our sacred energy being mad about this or trying to dismantle systems that have no interest in changing, we must turn our energies inward, unchaining ourselves from the very things and people who continue to tell us we aren't whole. This is how we create real change within ourselves. With these changes, we are better able to show up for not only ourselves but also the world, and especially the oppressed within it. We don't need to bypass the real truths of our trauma, our marginalization, or our histories, so many of which extend back thousands of years into hardship and slavery and struggle.

You are the new genetic code. You are the one for whom the dark ocean beckons, asking you to turn off all the lies and the systems that have been programmed to disconnect you from yourself. You are the Divine. And in fact, you are a miracle: the odds that you would come to exist are only one in 400 trillion. You, Spiritual Baddie, are on this planet for a purpose, and from this moment forward, you will claim your power back.

# The Agreement

*Note:* See the QR code in the eye on the first and last pages of this book for many free offerings to support and guide you in this work, including a full agreement that you can edit and print.

*This is an agreement you make with yourself and Spirit. From now on, you will make a better effort to honor yourself by liberating the Divine Self. You agree to not give up on yourself. You agree to trust yourself and Spirit throughout your journey. You agree to create a life you love, a life that supports you through the most challenging moments.*

Place one hand on the hand image and the other hand on your heart. Take three deep breaths, and, when ready, say out loud or in your mind the following:

Today I claim all that is meant for me.

I will no longer play small because I am ready to take up space.

I choose myself unconditionally and radically.

I will not apologize for anyone's discomfort during my expansion.

I will prioritize and readjust my life to make space for myself.

I will be patient with my healing and rest when I need to.

## The Altar Within

I will love myself unconditionally even when it's hard.

I will listen to my intuition, acknowledge my Divinity, and honor my Spirit.

I am no longer settling. I will only accept my worth in all areas of life.

I will follow my joy and live my Divined life.

I will not force things to happen; I know that what is coming for me will come.

xxx

I will not allow anyone or anything to make me feel like I am not enough or whole or sacred.

# FAQ

*Can I practice the guidance in this book and not turn my back on my religion?*

Yes, of course, Diosa! Your religion and your current practice or beliefs do not have to change. In fact, this practice will make them even more personal and powerful in your daily life. It is meant to elevate your life, and, as with anything else, I encourage you to take from it what you want and skip on what you don't.

*Am I too young to practice this?*

No. You can't be too young (or too old) to take a journey that revolves around you, honie. I would have loved to have a book like this when I was younger; it would have saved me so much anguish and confusion.

*The freebies you offer via QR code, are they all really free? Is there a catch?*

They're free! There is no catch; please utilize them. I put a lot of time and energy into these freebies. They are directly connected to this practice and will help amplify your journey.

*Do I need a whole lot of time to make room for this practice?*

There is an adjustment of daily space that will have to go into this practice, depending on your personal needs and levels of support. We must prioritize ourselves because we are worthy of making space. Period.

*Do I need a lot of money to practice in this way?*

No. In fact, all you need is *you*. That's why I offer all the tools in this book for free. Even when I speak about investing in yourself, please keep in mind that not everyone reading this book is in the same financial circumstance. I also added resources via the QR code for services and tools that our community has contributed for Spiritual Baddies on a budget.

*When should I start this practice?*

ASAP! Do not put yourself off for another day, bestie! The goal here isn't perfection, it's progress. It's perfectly normal to start slow; that slow start will gain fuel and take off before you know it. Sticking to a practice is a concern for many, and I definitely tackle how to overcome issues with self-commitment.

*What exactly is self-worship? Sounds like a cult.*

We will talk about this more soon enough, but right now I can tell you what it isn't. It is not about entitlement or selfishness. It is not "evil," and it does not mean you are a narcissist. It isn't a free ticket to treat others like shit or think you are above others. It does not replace your religion or gods or goddesses. It is quite simply a return to the Divine, the miraculous energy that made you!

PART

# 1

# The Divine Self

Before we get into the practices for self-worshipping, discovering, and activism, I want to go over some important things that are often misunderstood when we talk about spiritual growth. These things are essential for you to acknowledge in your journey here on Earth and for your continued spiritual growth and ascension.

This book is a devotional. It is meant to be by your side, read and practiced at your own pace. I offer additional tools, content, and resources for you to use throughout the book via the QR code—you can find it in the eye on the first or last pages. This book will guide you on a journey with yourself, and there is a lot to process. So cherish the journey and be patient, be mindful, and, please, BFF, be present.

# Divine Self

The Divine Self is referenced a lot in the spiritual community. You may even find different variations of the meaning, but ultimately there is a collective agreement that the Divine Self is our deepest, most connected essence.

Through the ages, the Divine Self has gone by many names: the Higher Self, the inner self, Christ-consciousness, Spirit, soul, and others. I choose to use *Divine Self*, *Spirit*, and *soul* to represent this higher intelligence that directly comes from Divinity, the intuition we all talk about. Therefore, I believe that we all are intuitive beings. We all are Divine. And since our Spirit is simply an expression of God, in worshipping the self, we are ultimately worshipping Divinity and all that is. (I choose to use *Divinity* in place of the word *God*.)

You = Divine Self = Divinity = You, all in the same.

The Divine Self is the true self-essence and presence of the universe that dwells in your being; its intelligence is beyond anything you can comprehend with your human mind. When we plug into this intelligence, we connect more deeply with that Divine source. She is wise, unafraid, and full of joy, happiness, compassion, drive, unconditional love, creativity, and purpose. She represents our most authentic state of being, a state that can feel fleeting when disconnected from Divinity. And there is much in our culture that drives this sense of disconnection (and profits from it too!).

Ultimately, there is no separation between you and your Divine Self. You are the same, Divinely fused, always connected. Acknowledging this can radically change the way you see yourself, your healing, and your part in this magnificent life. No one owns Divinity, for she is uncontainable. No religion or person can claim her for themselves, for she exists in us all.

*I started to heal deeply when I fully acknowledged that I am whole and that my wholeness is Divine. Therefore, I cannot be broken. I am infused with the power of the Divine source anytime I choose to be present to its existence.*

The Divine Self is whole, embodied, and all-knowing. She is already within us because we are her. The more we cut the cords to the things we are not, the more her presence illuminates our human nature. Remember, we are not here to try to attain; we are here to remember.

*The Altar Within* approaches self-worship, self-discovery, the Divine Self, and all other foundations covered in this book differently from New Age spiritualities. The goal here is to bring you back to self and all that is, including showing up to fight for your communities against dominant capitalist values. I am not here to turn you into a spiritually bypassing practitioner with a God complex or a slave to the capitalist consumerism overtaking the spiritual and wellness spaces, a.k.a. the "wellness industry."

It is vital for us Spiritual Baddies to not take self-worship and turn it into individualism. Through our work, we must also consider all the systems of colonialism and capitalist society that cause the issues and trauma we face, the ones that have sent us seeking answers and help from the wellness industry. *The perpetrator cannot also be the healer.*

When one suffers, we all suffer. Whether you realize it or not, that is the essence of humankind, the interconnectedness of all things and all beings. This is why I cannot be someone who ignores the world and all that is happening. At the moment, my homeland, Cuba, is in a civil war; recently, my people took to the streets collectively for the first time in nearly sixty years, and it was the biggest rising of the Cuban people ever. All over the world, Cuban people are coming together in unity for our families and those in the streets being murdered, taken, and silenced by a dictatorship—a dictatorship that does not care for humanitarian intervention or its people. I will not ignore the cries of my people so I can sit in silence, and I will not sit back in child's pose and hide my eyes from the evil lurking among us.

As I type these words, my eyes are blurred from tears, tears that my siblings feel at a soul level, tears that acknowledge the suffering they have endured to propel them to put their lives on the line in the name of collective justice and freedom. #libertadparatodos #freedomforall

I will never take my privilege for granted. Connecting to the Divine Self has awakened me and allowed me to realize that my privilege is meant to help amplify the voices and hearts of the people who are oppressed and continuously ignored. My mother risked her life, coming to America in a shifty boat while pregnant with me. I cannot ever dismiss or overlook this because it was her fire, her Spirit, and her sacrifice that likely gave me a better life than I would have had if I had been born on my island.

When you honor and connect into the Divine Self in honest and authentic ways that align with your truth, you will be propelled into demanding a life that works with you and not against you or your communities.

*The true nature of my Divine Self isn't willfully ignorant to the systems in place that are hurting and murdering our people.*

When something awful happens or when you are triggered by heavy, painful, negative emotions, you can choose how you react. You can allow these emotions to get the best of you, or you can choose to become the observer from a deeper state of awareness. I know you're probably wondering how this is even possible.

How could I possibly move through big, ugly emotions without judging, labeling, or feeling shame? You might have tried to do this before and, within seconds, the observer went out the window and you were back to feeling all the feelings. But that's because you weren't tapping into your true power.

This is your Divine Self's superpower—once you begin to cultivate your connection to Divinity, you will begin to be compassionate with yourself and others, more loving, remaining peaceful and calm amid the chaos. This took me months to practice, but eventually, it started to become second nature to me. It takes a lot of self-awareness and self-honesty, but you can achieve it. We don't want to ignore our emotions no matter how negative they are; healing happens when we see ourselves as we are.

Connecting with and devoting yourself to the Divine Self will help you resolve the cognitive dissonances created by capitalism, which is designed to divide and exploit our communities for profit. Capitalism creates an individualistic mindset and a separation of community, which can be seen in many of those people who practice New Age spirituality, whereas the Divine Self reminds you that there is no separation or hierarchy.

Systemic racism and discrimination within spiritual communities and wellness spaces harms BBIPOC most of all. It is a form of violence that keeps people of color from profoundly healing or easily accessing healing spaces, tools, and services. Many BBIPOC are battling real-life fear, stress, anxiety, anger, and grief (to name a few challenges) and are continuously forced out of or are blocked from our Divine Selves. For many years, this system of oppression has also made it more difficult for us to realize our true power and the power of unity within our own communities and spiritual realms.

Systemic oppression negatively impacts the physical, mental, and spiritual well-being and growth of BBIPOC communities. Regarding racism and discrimination, systemic oppression refers to the social policies, institutions, and structures that serve to oppress people of color. These systems and policies instituted by the settler-colonists continue to put marginalized groups at a disadvantage in all areas of their lives, including mental, physical, and spiritual health. They took away our cultures, religions, practices, and truths, replacing them with those of the colonizers, which were created to play us like a chess game that slowly continues to break us down. But where they fail is in acknowledging the mighty fire we have within us that cannot be extinguished by anything or anyone. It is our birthright. Our Divine Spirit. Nothing can destroy our Spirits.

Spiritual practices, beliefs, and wellness spaces that follow the old systems are just differently packaged, aesthetically driven marketing copy that still harms in the same ways. This is why the Divine Self can be the salve to modern hypercapitalism. Remembering and restoring our Divinity disrupts systemic oppression and decolonizes spirituality. When one of us wakes up, it ripples into our communities, helping to wake others. And this continues until we are all standing in the power of our Divine selves, collectively showing up for one another to fight against injustices, racism, and oppression.

*Remembering helps us to observe who we are and witness the things and people that are sabotaging us. It gives us access to a reflection of the self and all that does not belong to or support us.*

Your Divine Self is your Spiritual BFF! It is your inner guidance, your intuition, and it is pulling you, speaking to you, and sending you messages if you can find enough stillness to listen. Your Divine Self has your back, looks out for you, and would never steer you wrong. Yet so many of us still ignore and question her. We're so distracted by the loud noises and bright lights of our lives that we can't hear her whispering to us. But no worries; the more we release the parts of ourselves that aren't in alignment with our Divinity, the more we will know our Divine Selves.

Your intuition knows her shit. How many times have you felt an overwhelming feeling or even a nagging feeling that tells you, "No, honie, don't do it," or "Bestie, walk the other way"? My Divine Self has saved my life countless times. Living in the world that I grew up in, she was everything to me, my nurturer, my hero, my homegirl, my saving grace.

Have you ever just known something without knowing why? For example, when I was pregnant with my youngest one, four weeks before his due date, I was sitting at home with my then two-year-old, watching TV on New Year's Eve. We were alone and had no plans to leave the house. I started to feel an overwhelming sense of anxiety; it was hitting me hard and fast.

I barely could breathe as my little one told me, "Mommy, calm down. Are you okay?"

"Calm down, calm down," I heard echoing through the room in his sweet little voice. I gathered myself, sat down, closed my eyes, and asked, What are you trying to tell me? Instantly, I felt an urgency to save my baby. I didn't have any pains, no contractions, no discomfort; it was all Spirit alerting me to seek help.

I called my doctor, who said I was overreacting. He then told me it was New Year's Eve and that he was with family. He assured me I was fine and that my baby was too. For just a moment, I tried to tell myself, "Everything is okay, Juliet," but then, boom, the rush of urgency filled me with even more loudness as I started to sweat profusely. I then called my mother, who lived a few blocks away. She instantly felt something was wrong as well. She ran over, and we took off to the hospital in a taxi. Once there, the nurses told me that I was fine and had no signs of labor.

However, I did not back down and demanded that they check my baby. It turned out my baby was drowning. They did an emergency C-section, and he came out blue and full of water. He would have died if I'd ignored my Divine Self that night. Now, this is a bit extreme, but I assure you that no matter how big or small a situation, your Divine Self shows up whether or not you recognize her.

Working on connecting more intently to my Divine Self has amplified all of my gifts, especially my bullshit radar. And it will amplify yours as well. Prepare yourself, magical one. We are lighting you up! And by *we*, I mean our spiritual teams. Our ancestors and guides. Our spiritual teachers here on Earth and those in the beyond. I am no savior, and I am no better than you; I am simply a vessel through which Divinity is working to help you wake up, live your Divined life, and worship the very ground you walk on.

## Where Is She Though?

Oh, bestie, I know, I know. I am not going to deny that at times, it is hard to connect with the Divine Self. Or when you're deep in your feelings, it can feel practically impossible to step into the observer space. And there are times when we all feel alone, lost, and hopeless. I've been there more often than I want to admit, but, just as I realized in my vision, remember that we don't have to live in the dark ocean. The Divine Self always arrives to pull us out if we're willing to extend our hand, to trust in the great energy flowing through us. Those rare moments don't have to be so rare; you can plug back in and experience the magic all the damn time.

When I was a senior in high school, many of my classmates did not know that I was homeless. For the last three months of my senior year and for sixteen months, three days, four hours, and twelve minutes after that, I lived wherever I could find shelter. I started to count because I needed something to root me in the belief that I would overcome this, as long as I took it one day at a time. So each day, I made sure to do something that would help me move forward and not stay stuck in my situation. I was determined to not let that storyline dictate my future. I was going to make sure my story continued and that it continued with the grace and magic of Divinity.

It was hard, so very hard, to keep a smile on my face. It was even harder to stay grateful, let alone keep the faith. There were many times I worked a few days in a row with as little as three hours of sleep. I moved from place to place to keep my energy from becoming stagnant. I burned weeds as my form of cleansing and bathed in the city's river. Once in college (yes, I went to college homeless, with a full-ride because of my high grades), I joined the swim team because they practiced in the early mornings and I could shower there. I slept in the school closets until I was caught. I ate leftovers from my friends' plates, offering to clear the cafeteria table after everyone was finished eating. I grabbed clothes from the lost and found and dived into donation drop-off bins around the city to collect donated clothes and shoes. I wore a size 11 sneaker for a few months even though I'm a size 9.

Then, in the moments that I wanted to give up, Divinity showed up. She would wag her finger at me and say, "Uh-uh, honie! Have you forgotten the shit you have pulled through? Have you forgotten the blood you have spilled, the flesh that's been beaten, the tears you have collected? Keep going, BFF! Keep following the path; I got you."

And so, I followed the path wherever it led me—one day at a time. Little by little, I saved enough to rent small rooms to crash in, buy better clothes, and get better jobs. Connections and alignments began to appear, and, before I knew it, here I was, with all the abundance any girl could ask for, a second chance at life, a deep and intimate love with my partner of eleven years, and two children that have given me so much love, it has surpassed the love I wasn't shown before. It has given me a delicious awe for myself and my faith and a full-on devotion to my Divinity.

It is safe to surrender your fears, doubts, and worries, for you are Divinely protected and guided. Look to the moon and the stars above you, the Earth below you, and the Divine within. Everything is working in your favor.

**2**

**DEVOTIONAL**

# Bypassing Spiritual Bypassing

If you believe that life is all light and love, you live in a delusion, hermana. There is no light without shadow, and you know this if you have genuinely retreated into the self and found true stillness. Our fierceness was born out of the shadow that dwells in silence, and because of it, we are stronger, wiser, and more powerful. Divinity created light, and she also created darkness, equally out of love and purpose. I don't need to question her because if I am to trust anyone or anything, it is Divinity. It is man who decided to use the term *shadow* against us as a weapon to dim our lights and to be ashamed of our pain.

Life does not exist only to make you happy or to be in a state of bliss and creation; it also exists to dismantle, disrupt, and redesign. The natural state of life is Divinity, and Divinity isn't any one thing. It is wild and free, as we should be. Everyone, at some point, experiences challenges. And I understand now that the way to heal ourselves and get through these challenging times is through the essence we were created from.

Now, let's address something truly important: the notion that darkness/black is evil. Because evil is very real, and it isn't a creation of Divinity; it is a creation of man. Man said that black is bad and white is good. These concepts were interwoven into the dominant culture and our spiritual ideas, confusing us into giving evil power and stripping our personal power and innate magic. Your shadow is not evil; your shadow is Divine, as is your light. Darkness/black isn't bad; it is powerful, and without this acknowledgment, you can't truly plug back into Divinity. Instead, you will remain connected to racist and colonized belief systems. These systems show their faces in wellness practices that simultaneously spiritually bypass

*Spiritual bypassing* is a "tendency to use spiritual ideas and practices to sidestep or avoid facing unresolved emotional issues, psychological wounds, and unfinished developmental tasks," according to the man who developed the term, John Welwood, a Buddhist teacher and psychotherapist, who first shared the concept in the early 1980s.

Spiritual bypassing is shoved into our subconscious on a daily basis, through social media and throughout the world in which we live. New Age spirituality has taken over like a drug, though one that temporarily feels good and then hits you with a reality check from all those dirty little side effects. If you ask me, it's become a franchise of cultural appropriation and half-assing your healing all in the name of Good Vibes Only. #youcantfoolspirit

Spiritual bypassing limits our personal development and healing, and it can interrupt our spiritual growth. Bypassing is a way of hiding behind spiritual beliefs and practices that keep us from acknowledging what we are feeling—dismissing emotions and swiping left on them—which only disconnects us from our Divine Selves.

Instead of protecting the self, you are causing more harm. This does not create a better you, a more positive you, or a world in harmony with others. Instead, it glosses over problems and issues, leaving them to fester and build without any actual resolution.

Bypassing occurs when you turn away from your lived experiences, denying them, ignoring them, calling them something other than what they are. Most of us are so used to bypassing that we may not even realize when we are doing it. Many others are afraid to face deep wounds and don't want to risk allowing raw human connection with the self or others to avoid being hurt. Engaging in spiritual bypassing can ultimately hinder your growth, expansion, and healing. But don't be too hard on yourself if this is something you have been doing; it may be that a little spiritual bypassing got you through some hard times.

It's easy to fall into old habits, especially when you are trying to cope with something difficult; trust me, I know, BFF. But by actively avoiding spiritual bypassing, you can make spirituality a practice that will help you thrive and plug back into Divinity.

# Bypassing Spiritual Bypassing

When it's stripped of spiritual bypassing, spirituality can be a positive force in your life. Remember that you are not just a spiritual being; you are also a human being. You can't be whole without acknowledging your *whole* self.

Spiritual bypassing examples:

○ avoiding feelings that make you uncomfortable
○ avoiding emotions that are not deemed "positive" or "good vibes only"
○ pretending that things are fine when they are clearly not
○ believing that you are only a spiritual being and that, therefore, humanness doesn't apply
○ being overly optimistic
○ believing that a traumatic event must serve as a "learning experience," so it is what it is
○ using defense mechanisms such as denial and repression
○ believing that those who suffer or those who are going through something aren't spiritual people and are negative
○ believing in idealism or perfectionism
○ ignoring real life in the name of spirituality
○ projecting your own negative feelings onto others
○ thinking that people can overcome their problems through positive thinking or doing spiritual practices like meditation
○ thinking that taking action to support world issues is going to lower your frequency
○ believing that everything happens for a reason

Spiritual bypassing isn't always bad; in times of severe distress, it can temporarily relieve complex emotions. However, it can be damaging when used as a long-term strategy to suppress emotions, experiences, and problems. Some side effects of spiritual bypassing are:

○ anxiety
○ unexplained stress on the mind, body, Spirit

○ unexplained sickness and health issues

○ blind allegiance to leaders, influencers, and spiritual teachers

○ codependency

○ control problems, especially when one is obsessed with perfection

○ disregard for personal responsibility

○ feelings of shame, disgust, and self-hate

○ feeling "chosen" (a.k.a. spiritual narcissism)

I've worked with thousands of people in spiritual communities. In this work, one thing has often come up: people feel shame for feeling anything other than positivity. For instance, feelings of sadness, anger, loneliness, jealousy, or annoyance are considered in conflict with spirituality. So rather than deal with their feelings, people use spiritual bypassing as a crutch, failing to take responsibility for the actions that are birthed out of ignoring those emotions.

To connect with your Divine Self, you first have to learn how to acknowledge your feelings and embrace them. Allow yourself to process and feel fully, including the painful hurts; it does not make you weak or less spiritual. On the contrary, it makes you whole, stronger, and wiser, and it sets you on a path of transcendence, allowing you to embody your most authentic self. #magicalaf

This also applies when it comes to other people. Spiritual bypassing can cause us to bypass other people's emotions, experiences, and hardships. Looking down at or judging other people for expressing justifiable emotions like anger, fear, and sadness is a form of spiritual bypassing. Just as you shouldn't suppress your own emotions, you shouldn't dismiss other people's either.

I call myself a Spiritual Activist, and I can't avoid the very real connection between spirituality, world issues, and politics. I feel, deep in my soul, that we can change the world for the better if we work on our self-development—mind, body, and soul. Having a practice that helps your spiritual growth and healing will also help us all show up and evolve as human and spiritual beings—beings that want a more just, more peaceful, and safer world for us *all*.

"You are not weak; there is nothing wrong with you. Your reaction is an appropriate reaction to living in a violent and unsustainable system and way of life. Spiritually ground BUT do not spiritually BYPASS."

—Dr. Rosales Meza (Give her a follow on IG @dr.rosalesmeza to access her work on decolonizing.)

Justifying suffering is another form of spiritual bypassing and one that boils my blood every time I see and hear it. People always find ways to justify not taking action—from "It's the natural plan of the universe" to "It's as God intended" to "Everything happens for a reason." When people say these things, I want them to offer that to my five-year-old self while she was being sexually abused by a grown man. Would you have justified my suffering because "It is what it is"? I assume that the nine apartments on my floor of the seven-story building I lived in thought that my screams weren't their responsibility either because, according to such explanations, this was not their problem. #fuckyou

No one should get a free pass to accept things as they are. Spirituality requires that we focus on what we can do to make a difference. Yes, some situations may be outside of our control or extremely difficult to face, but in all situations, change can be made and lives can be saved. Remember, you are the greatest expression of the Divine, and therefore Divinity works through you.

## How to Avoid Spiritual Bypassing

First, we must acknowledge that we comprise different parts that make us whole— mind, body, Spirit. These parts make the self, and they all work together to create our magical, transcendent, holistic human experience. I am not going to deny that this can be hard AF, and I can say, from lived experience, that bypassing my shadow parts was a way to survive my traumatic experiences. I had to undo so much to heal what was hidden away.

For some of us, it can be painful, uncomfortable, and even scary, but embracing your truth will release you from what doesn't serve you and from what's holding you back from your spiritual growth. Your truth is the key to your Divine Self.

We will dive deeper into this in the self-discovery section, but know this: you are not alone in this work. I got you, BFF! #spirtualhug

For now, try this:

○ Cut the cords with your "good vibes only" belief system. You are a spiritual, magical, Divine being even when you are not in "high vibes only" mode. You can still manifest and tap into Divinity because it is your Divine right. And the more you acknowledge the whole you, the more you will develop an authentically positive mindset, manifesting a higher-vibing version of yourself—not one rooted in charlatans and false prophets, but one born from your own profound healing and Divine Self.

○ Remind yourself that negative thoughts and feelings serve a purpose. The goal is not to avoid having negative thoughts; it is to use those thoughts to inspire positive actions. Your shadow propels deep healing, illuminating your Divine truth and spiritual growth.

○ If you find that sitting with or facing your emotions is too heavy or too painful, shift your perspective to mothering yourself. Be compassionate and patient. Emotions have a purpose, and they will take you to the parts of yourself that are triggering the areas of your lived experience that created these emotions in the first place. Travel slowly with them; allow your Divine intelligence to guide you through them.

*If what you practice grows stronger, imagine what would happen if you focused that practice onto the self.*

# Blood, Roots, and Bones

In order to develop a spiritual practice that feeds our minds, bodies, and Spirits, to create Divine medicine for strength, renewal, grounding, and growth, we must integrate our humanness. Our elemental nature. Our connection to the Earth and the ancestors who came before us. Our very natures allow for death and rebirth and evolving, each time we shed what does not serve us. Just as there isn't a separation from you and divinity, there isn't a separation from you and the Earth or the Ancestors. You are the whole package, bestie.

As I mentioned before, you have a spiritual team, and that team also includes your ancestors and this magnificent Earth, Divinity's greatest gift to living beings. We are not alone; we are guided, protected, and loved. And you are the one your ancestors have been waiting for, the one that can end generational cycles of trauma and violence and human hurt. Your ancestors want for you what they could not have for themselves. Your sacred lineage requires that you cut the cord to the things that do not serve you.

Today, we have so much more access to tools, resources, and time, so we can heal and grow in ways our ancestors couldn't. And if your ancestors were enslaved like mine, you have the freedom they prayed for, the freedom they died for—the freedom to choose, to be able to be who you are, to be able to worship as you desire, and to be able to grow from insight, access to information, wisdom, and connectedness. We betray our ancestors when we don't honor their sacrifices, when we don't embrace the great and immortal freedom in which we live.

*You are who your ancestors have been waiting for.*

I speak on our connection to the Earth in my book *Plant Witchery*. If you don't have it already, get it, BFF! There is so much in there that will help you realize your part in the sacred connection we have to Earth. We are Earth. We are nature. This is our humanness, our flesh, our roots, and our bones. We are carrying the blood of our ancestors within this sacred temple. You are a fucking Diosa, my friend.

The more you do this work, the more you will begin to see that everything in your life is one massive web of interconnectedness—all parts working together, as they should, to bring you into a state of harmony with self and life. You will start to see and feel the signs within and all around you. You don't have to be a seer, or know who your ancestors were, or be able to hear Spirits, to have a direct connection with Spirit.

*Remember, you are the Altar.*

Before we continue, let's get some misleading beliefs out of the way. Just because you haven't seen or heard your ancestors does not mean they are not communicating with you. Way too many people get stuck on this being the goal or believe this makes someone more gifted than another. What are you expecting? Lighting to strike suddenly? Do yourself a favor, step out of the fantasy world that magic paints on TV, and give yourself a chance to understand and witness real magic all around you.

We all have ancestors, and we all are directly connected to them. Yes, some of us, like me, are able to hear and see them, but that doesn't make me any better or more worthy. It does not mean I'm chosen or extra special. All it means is that we are all unique in our own ways. The connection you have with your ancestors transcends time and space, so the way you connect may not look or feel the same as someone else connecting. It also doesn't mean that you're incapable of opening these gifts yourself. You will be surprised at the abilities you will amplify and manifest by connecting back to self. You are the one wielding power.

Your ancestors are a part of you. No matter what. You can't ever lose that connection, even if you don't know who they are because records weren't kept adequately, or your family was removed from their ancestral land, or you were adopted and don't have information about your birth parents. Whether you know them or not, the ancestors rejoice through you. They want us to fulfill our purpose and live our Divined life. It is through you that they can see their prayers answered. They want for you to heal, rest, be present in joy, spiritually grow, and be the baddest bitch there ever was.

*May the voices of my ancestors spill from my lips; may their prayers fill my Spirit and their wisdom move my heart. For I am the vessel in which they conjure revolutions and brew powerful medicine. They live magically through me.*

When connecting and honoring our ancestors both from Spirit and Blood, you acknowledge another essential part of you. Because beyond our family relations, there are also the ancestors of nature, the Earth, oceans, rivers, trees, mountains, and animals. Then there are those you choose to honor or worship like goddesses, gods, deities, saints, people, and so on. Everyone praises and worships differently, and there isn't a right or wrong way of doing it. Even if you follow a particular religion or practice with rules and ways of doing things, you can still adjust it to suit you in a way that feels more authentic.

An issue that is rarely addressed is understanding how to communicate with ancestors who were colonizers. If you live on stolen land, your people may have historically appropriated, ravaged, and destroyed Native cultures and practices. People often ask me if these colonizers are good to have as ancestors, and honestly, they are asking someone whose ancestors suffered at the hands of theirs, so to me, the answer is no. I would much rather see you connect to those that were good people. Not ancestors who raped, tortured, murdered, and forcefully stole our lands. Instead, focus on ancestors that are going to help you grow, heal, and find your truth.

It's a little like finding a chosen family who supports you, versus continuing to support a toxic biological family who you cannot trust. We can find the ancestors

23

who best support our work and cut off the ones who perpetuated the violence and traumas of our present day.

But also, you can help repair your ancestors' violence, this is the true nature of reparative work, to heal generations forward from the pains of generations past.

We all must find loving and caring companions that can guide us through our journeys. You have them! They are with you; all you need is yourself and moments of reflection to connect with those that are here to support your healing, growth, and ascension. Just like living people, there are the good, and there are the not-so-good ancestors. Cut those cords that do not serve you or your lineage.

We deserve to move forward into a new world where we all respect, acknowledge, and hold space for one another, no matter what race, color, religion, or sex we are, how we identify, or who we love, marry, or fuck. We are all diverse and unique, and honoring that is honoring Divinity. The Divine does not make mistakes with her creations, and she made no mistakes in how she made you.

Diseases like racism, homophobia, transphobia, and white supremacy aren't Divine; they are man-made, and we have the power to eradicate them. If we can look within ourselves and connect to our truths, we will see that despite our differences, we are all the same.

Change can't happen in this world if we continue to point fingers and dwell on the things that keep us separated. There has to be unity, and by *unity*, I mean we have to do the work to honor one another's voices, acknowledge injustices, and stand up for one another, even if it means we start revolutions. By turning a blind eye to what was done and what is still being done to our brothers and sisters, our Earth, our waters, our animals, and our human rights, we deepen our disconnection with the Divine.

We all are armed with the tools to help save this Earth and one another. We were born during these times for a reason, to *rise*. And this is not to say that just because we come together we have to be in community with one another. The truth is, we don't. I stand for you because I honor you, your humanity, and your innate right to be free, safe, and protected. I love you because you are the essence of Spirit and all that is.

We can be in unity without being in the same community. But instead, we often complicate the work, losing focus on the things that matter the most—our survival, our joy, our peace, our reclamation, and our sovereignty. In unity, we can harmoniously live among one another, no matter who we are or where we come from.

*Sorry, but I'm busy making my ancestors proud. #notsorry*

Just as in any meaningful relationship, our connections with our ancestors need love and care. In many cultures like my own, your relationship with your ancestors is crucial to your everyday life and spiritual growth. For us, it's a lifestyle and one that we take very seriously, devoting time each day to honor them. Doing so does not have to be complicated; there are simple yet powerful ways to honor and grow your relationship with the ancestors. They can be a vital source of nourishment, medicine, and wisdom, connecting us to the Divine Self within.

## Sacred Space

Before you continue deeper into this practice, I suggest you find or create a space or Altar dedicated to your ancestors. Intentionally care for and maintain it to ensure your ancestors have a place to rest, convene, and commune with you. There are many reasons people keep Ancestral Altars, but one of the main reasons I recommend having one is so you can create a practice in which you are reminded of those that came before you, instilling gratitude every time you see it.

This is a space where you can honor them through prayer, connection, making offerings, and showing respect. This space can be as grand or as simple as you want. It's the intention that counts. You don't even have to have an Altar if you choose not to; as I mentioned earlier, you are the Altar! All you really need is yourself to connect with the great Spirits around you.

I'm not here to tell you how to create or keep your Altars or sacred spaces because, again, we all have different preferences, but here are a few things to consider including:

○ images of your ancestors
○ items that belonged to them
○ images of the land they lived on
○ flowers, foods, candy, drinks, or anything that they enjoyed
○ the elements
○ cultural representations
○ music, poems, stories, or books that they may have loved or that represent them

Keep your Altar or sacred space clean and clutter-free, and dust it often. If you add water, make sure to change it regularly. If you add food as an offering, don't let it sit for more than twenty-four hours, as it can spoil. Fruits that have not been opened or cut can be left until they start to ripen fully. Flowers should be replaced once they start to die; keep life going on the Altar.

The options are endless. Note that if you do not have the means to make a detailed Altar, a simple candle and photo will do. Don't have an image of them? Look for images that represent them, or skip the pictures and write a letter instead, directing it to your ancestors. You can do whatever you desire. Tapping into what your ancestors prefer is also one of the best ways to understand what they are trying to say.

## Get Out to Nature

Nature is ancestral, and it is home to us all. You can't go wrong with worshipping the Earth and her nature Spirits. I love to go out to nature all the time; it is my church. I spend my time foraging, planting, and swimming in rivers, oceans, and lakes. But I especially love to sit under or by a waterfall and meditate or just be present. Hiking is one of my forms of medicine; there isn't a trail I've turned away from yet. If hiking interests you, keep in mind that most places offer hikes at different levels, from beginner to experienced. Don't let lack of experience scare you away from getting into the deep of Mother Earth. It is one of the most magical ways to connect with her. Get out there and spend time with our nature Spirits. Honor, cherish, clean, heal, and protect them. In return, Mother Earth will offer healing and renewal. She will reset your Spirit. Nature instantly connects you to your roots. The Earth is your home, an innate birthright, and the more we spend time with her, the more we feel connected to our truth and essence.

## Synchronicity and Signs

Direct contact with your ancestors and the Earth does not have to always be through rituals and ceremonies. As I said, you don't even have to have an Altar, if that is what you prefer. It can be as simple as allowing yourself to be in tune with your inner and outer world. Synchronicity and spiritual messages are all around us. They can show up in numbers, colors, shapes, nature, animals, dreams, and people. All it takes is for us to stop and notice them. Acknowledge them when you do, and as time goes on you will notice that they become more prominent.

When we ignore these signs, however, they stop trying to reach us in this way. All you have to do is ask them to keep trying, and once they see you are paying attention, they will continue to try to connect with you.

Remember: you are the key to how you connect. This acknowledgement is vital in your relationship with your truth and with all that is. Don't get caught up in the aesthetics and 'grams circulating on the web. You do not need anything other than yourself to create magic and manifest what you desire. You are already whole, you carry everything you need, and you are capable and worthy of living a Divined life that is aligned with who you are. You are the source of your spiritual growth and healing.

# Sacred Truths

Living your Divined life is a beautiful way to honor your ances-tors. Remember that they are within and living through you. Your ancestors are allies in your journey to remembering and re-claiming your power. Through healing, self-care, and love, through honoring and worshipping your temple (which we will get to in the next part of this book), you will find your way to connect intimately with them and celebrate them.

There are also real actions we can take to honor them; for in-stance, I am an activist. I have been a leader in bringing awareness to my Taino ancestors' truth. The lies about them being extinct have brainwashed even the people who are their descendants. Continuing my ancestors' traditions, ceremonies, and rituals, speaking their na-tive language, and working with the medicinal plants they used keeps them alive. My family in Cuba has long kept these Ancestral Medicines and traditions that they passed down to us. Acknowledg-ing my Indigenous roots is a sacred way for me to bring respect to them and honor them.

As part of my tribute to them, I also protect and fight for the Earth and her lands, animals, and waters. You can choose ways to do things that bring honor to your ancestors. Do what feels right for you, but know that when we connect to their traditions, their truths, and their power, we connect deeper to the Divine Self within.

PART

# Self-Worship

Here we are, best friend! Consider me your Spiritual Baddie BFF. I am so excited to go on this journey with you and so very proud of you for saying yes to Spirit.

In modern-day spirituality, you hear a lot about doing the work, and it usually looks like this:

the work (healing) = self-love + acceptance + forgiveness = enlightenment, wisdom, better you, Divine Self

But there is a flaw in this order; you see, doing the work is fucking hard, as I mentioned, even triggering. This leaves many people stuck in the pain stage, and because they think it's supposed to be all ancestral wisdom and crystal powers, they give up when they realize that this shit is also hard. No one wants to bring up past traumas while at the same time finding a way to love themselves because it's exhausting. Meanwhile, they buy into the lie that it's good vibes only or Spirit won't grant you your wishes. #overit

Your Spirit has faith in you, and that faith is what keeps you going and trying over and over again. You are not doing it wrong, and you are not broken. Just to sum it up, this is what you have been asked to do: heal all of the past, find your truth, find your purpose, and then throw in healing ancestral karma, make sure to stay positive, keep a smile on your face, eat this way and not that way, reprogram yourself by attaining this and that, and manifest yourself into your better self. Oh, and also deal with real life-hardships and mental chaos. Ugh! Pass me my cannabis and some chocolate and call it a fucking day. No, my loves, we're going to do this differently. We acknowledge all of you, the shadows included.

# What Is Self-Worship?

Self-worship is a revolution. It is liberation. It is a fuck-you to everything and everyone who has ever made you feel less than, not worthy, or not whole. It is a reverence to Spirit and devotion to yourself. Self-worship is vital for abolishing patriarchal rule, waking the reclamation of your story, and finding your voice newly embodied by power and truth.

When you worship yourself, you honor Divinity (God)(Goddess) through the very vessel she created. The most powerful way to worship Divinity, Spirit, and ancestors is through radically and unapologetically loving and caring for yourself. You can believe whatever you want, worship whoever you like, be in whatever religion you wish, and still self-worship.

When you dedicate yourself to this work, you are unchaining yourself from the supremacy-rooted belief that you aren't good enough and from the dominance of colonialism, which has isolated you from your Divine Self. It's no wonder that most of us are lost, blindly seeking and battling with faith, especially when life becomes hard to navigate.

Self-worship is a deep and authentic exploration of self, which also requires acknowledging *all the things* that live within the depths of you—facing your wounds, trauma, not-so-pretty emotions, and triggers. It means breaking the chains of spiritual bypassing and digging into your emotions and the realities around you to better transmute your lived experiences in a healthy way instead of suppressing, ignoring, or make-believing they aren't there. Bestie, they are there, and it's okay.

It doesn't mean you are any less spiritual if you don't fit into the hierarchy of spiritual practices that vomit "excessive optimism" to make you believe you're more "woke." When we ignore the hardships of real life, we end up spiritually bypassing other people's hardships as well. These beliefs separate you from not only your truths but also community. Community is the medicine of the soul. In community, we are united, and when we are united, we are powerful. It is a delusion to live in "light and love," thinking that is how we evolve and bring forth a new world. In truth, the only way to illuminate our Spirits and create a better world for all of us is to acknowledge our shadows. You can't do that if you wear sparkly unicorn cotton-candy glasses that block reality's entire spectrum of colors and shades.

34

You came here to have a human experience, and you can't have a human experience if you ignore that you are human. And, BFF, being human means that sometimes life sucks and hurts.

Self-worship brings you back to Spirit, and in doing so, you are coming back home to self, to your heart, to the place from which Spirit leads you. It is nearly impossible to be heartless in this space, to not realize or acknowledge when hurt, harm, and disrespect is present. It calls for you to tap into your own roots and Indigenous practices, it calls for you to question why you are practicing in a certain way, and it calls for you to dig deeper into where those spiritual practices come from. It asks that you look at every detail of self and your life.

Today, we see so many blatant appropriations of ancient sacred practices, with people using the word *appreciation* to excuse their exploitation and profiting off of other people's cultures. You can't come into my home and take whatever you want just because you like it, no matter how you phrase it, it is still stealing. And when people capitalize off of the very people they say they appreciate, they are stealing.

You can't say you are not responsible for what your ancestors did while you are not only continuing to benefit from it but also perpetuating the belief systems that drove those ancestors' behaviors. Believing in light and love and good vibes only and then supporting practices and beliefs that continue to harm BBIPOC makes you a contributor to the violence. #thefuck

Let me share an example of this with you. I was invited to a spiritual retreat at which they hoped my Taino family, Higuayagua, would come and do some sort of

# What Is Self-Worship?

Ceremony where we share our medicine, wisdom, and practices to help people connect, heal, and cleanse. I am a bohuiti of my Higuayagua family, and part of my role as a medicine keeper is to protect our sacred medicine, ceremonies, and rituals and carry on our practices for generations to come. Naturally, I felt that I needed to know more about the retreat before getting my sisters and brothers into a situation that wasn't aligned with them and, especially, to make sure that our elders would be safe.

I decided to go to this retreat with my mother to check it out. The location was beautiful—it was in nature and by a gorgeous body of water. There were acres of land, and all the invited Indigenous native tribes were spread out into different locations. There was a map and a schedule to help you know what was coming up next and where. At first, I was excited and felt blessed to be able to experience the medicine of all these different tribes, especially the Mexican elders, who passed by me as we were setting up. They shared with me that my energy was enormous, that I would be a force in the world. Wow, what a way to fill my heart and eyes with optimism.

But as I followed this map and took a good look around, I became extremely disappointed. Makeshift stages and tents were set up on an open field where the sun beamed down without mercy, leaving many of the Indigenous guests exposed and exhausted from the heat. The schedule revealed that for a few days, elders from all over the world would have to continuously conduct their ceremonies and rituals for the crowds of people who purchased tickets to be there. In my defense, I had no clue what these ticket prices were because I was invited. If I did, that would have been the first red flag. The prices were so ridiculously high that only a privileged person could afford them.

Before I could say a word, my mother turned to me and glared into my eyes. Without saying a word, I understood her Spirit. I could feel her pain, I could feel her anger, and I could feel my ancestors pulling at my core, saying, "This is wrong." All of the people doing the ceremonies and offerings were of color, but all of the paying guests were white and were wearing feathers in their hair; some even wore headdresses, and many had on face paint.

This wasn't even what made me upset. What was really heartbreaking was the fact that the very people who came from these cultures, this medicine, and this wisdom weren't there to experience it—the BBIPOC who deserved to be there and receive healing were not present because the retreat was organized in a way that would not be accessible to most BBIPOC.

I walked to where the Mexican Medicine Woman was setting up; she was a Curandera elder of a tribe I will not name because at the time, I didn't know I would be writing about it and didn't ask for permission. She walked up to me and put her hand on my stomach and grabbed it tight and said, "Esto que sientes aquí es una mala dirección de cómo usar tu don como vidente, pero aquí—" she placed her hand gently on my heart—"es de donde te está guiando tu Espíritu. Deja que te guíe." She told me, *This feeling you have right here [my stomach] is a misdirection of how to use your gift as a seer. Your Spirit is guiding you from here [my heart]. Let it guide you.*

I started to cry, and out of nowhere she slapped me with a huge bundle of herbs and poured a bucket of the cleansing waters she created over my head. Before I knew it, I was smoking tobacco from every part of my body and then stepping over fire. #ultimatelimpia

Wow! I felt like we were in a dance in the realms beyond this one. She, like me, was a seer. She began speaking to me as if she were speaking directly to my soul. What she told me is sacred, and so I will keep it with me. But I can tell you that my heart led me to where I am now. And nearly everything she said has manifested, and I expect that the rest of it is coming.

But not seeing any of the people who would benefit from such a retreat in attendance there broke me. It opened my eyes to the violent ignorance toward Indigenous healing. And it blew my mind that the more than three hundred people present did not have any concerns over the blatant disrespect, appropriation, and profit being made off these sacred souls. We cannot take from the elders and our ancestors without ensuring that the medicine is being offered to all, especially those from which the medicine was born.

Wake up, besties! Your mission is here, on Earth, not gazing at the stars and dreaming of another home. This is your home now, this is where your presence is needed, and this is where your glorious star power can contribute to propelling this world into a better place, and you cannot do that by ignoring the things, people, and systems that keep us oppressed. We're not here by accident. And we are living during these revolutionary times because we have a part to play in shifting and saving this world.

We need to be *present*; we need to show up for ourselves and each other and give a fuck about humanity, the Earth, and dismantling the spiritual and wellness spaces and industries until they are for the people—for *all the people*.

Take a deep breath, BFF. This is a lot to process. But through self-worship, you will begin to step into your power. Your body, mind, and Spirit want to heal deeply and intimately with you, but they cannot do that if you are continuing to harm yourself and others. Spirit wants to feel loved, cared for, understood, and fiercely protected by you. We cannot abandon each other. More than anything, we must join in community, we must speak up, and we must question everything, not so we can be "woke" but so we can all be healed.

*Self-worship should be a lifestyle that calls for liberatory political action to transform our socialization, where we question everything, especially our habits, patterns, and beliefs. It should redefine who you are, your goals, aspirations, values, and intentions, and allow you to take responsibility for your role in colonial systems of oppression while compassionately taking care of yourself.*

Self-worship liberates you from the commodification of self-care, self-love, and self-realization because radical self-care actually aids in dismantling the oppressor within and without. Many of the people selling courses, memberships, books, services, and products branded by "self-love," "self-care," "feminine power," and "goddess collectives" are profiting off of our traumas, experiences, and need for community. Meanwhile, those very communities are filled with people who dismiss our truth and spiritually bypass and willfully appropriate our cultures, medicine, and wisdom while not giving any fucks about our safety and need for societal change. #callthemout

These commodified healing practices are promoting colonialist, capitalist systems that are racist, privileged, and patriarchal and that in no way contribute to social justice or our collective spiritual, mental, physical, and emotional wellness. They promote self-care as a means to pleasure, to only feeling good or being in positive vibes, but self-care can also be painful, mundane, and not pretty, and it does not require you to have a good day every day. Self-care has become something you treat yourself with, a luxury because of how they sell it to you, but it doesn't just live in the simplistic acts and rituals of aesthetically beautiful baths, spa days, yoga, meditation, and so on (thought it can live in those things, too, as I'll soon describe). However, it also involves practical everyday tasks for which we are all responsible.

*Stop running from yourself. Eventually all that will be left are ashes trailing behind you, when you could be blazing with the stars instead. You are safe. You are protected. You are Divinely loved.*

Most days, I call it a win for self-worship when I remember to take my supplements, get my grocery shopping done, do the laundry, make sure my children are showered and don't smell like ass, finish watching my favorite Netflix series that makes me feel nostalgic, remind my husband how much I appreciate and love him, tend to the weeds in my garden, and make time to take a big breath of fresh air when I am feeling anxious or when I choose to just chill and do nothing because that is what I need at the moment.

But self-worship can also be doing the things that you are not used to implementing and that you may be uncomfortable with or don't consider fun or pleasurable. It could be setting boundaries with yourself and others, showing up authentically for yourself, or practicing self-honesty and accountability. Self-care can be having the self-discipline to get your sacred body to the gym or, if you're like me, to work out from home. Self-care can be getting in some meditation time or movement or including healthier foods in your daily meals. But it can also be taking time off when you need to rest and enjoying a piece of cake when you feel like it. You know better than anyone what feels good to you and what does not. It is time you start to trust your intuition. You already know what hasn't worked for you and what you need.

In self-worshipping, we take self-care and love to the next level. We become our own support system and build a powerful relationship with ourselves and Divine Spirit. We learn how to check ourselves, heal ourselves, and continuously grow spiritually. Not that we can't have outside support, which is super important, but you are now cultivating self-awareness and elevating intuition that can get you through the most challenging times. With self-worship, you finally have the power to release feelings of loneliness and of not feeling loved and supported.

We do not have to put ourselves in a box that is created to keep us from taking up space; we must take up space and not conform or bend our backs to a system that is not supporting our true liberation, one that has programmed us into thinking we are meant to be small, one that has us believing that we can only live and exist within white supremacy's systems and not beyond it, keeping many of us from dreaming big and exploring the possibilities waiting for us.

When you liberate the Divine, you find freedom within yourself. You become your biggest fan because you are 100 percent worthy of being loved by you. You will believe in yourself like you have never before, and, most importantly, you will brew the most delicious relationship with Divinity, a medicine to which you can turn to again and again as you deepen your healing. When we can take care of ourselves mentally, physically, and spiritually, we are also better able to show up in our truth and purpose for the world and in service to others, like our families, friends, and communities.

# Decolonizing Spirituality

I have come to realize the real work isn't about #overnighttransformation. The real work is decolonizing spirituality. In doing so, we not only create an authentic reaction to life and our own experiences, but we also dismantle the capitalist and toxic spiritual beliefs that have been buried in our subconscious. The real work asks that we remember who we are, calling back our energy, connecting into ancestry and heritage, reclaiming our ancient wisdom and medicine.

The real work is about getting rid of the guilt we feel for not always being positive, for the days we can barely make it out of our beds, for the days we scream inside our cars during our "breaks." To claim your Divine purpose, awaken your power, and protect your life force, you must unlearn and return to truth. No one can ever tell you again what your liberation looks like.

Decolonizing spirituality, "the work," requires that we reclaim our sacred sovereignty. That means when we don't want to be on, we get to turn ourselves off. Spiritual work is also resting, recuperating, and recovering. It looks like leading your life with Spirit, following your path with heart, and unraveling everything that doesn't serve you to make space for what does. Most especially, it looks like living our Divined lives for our ancestors, our grandmothers and grandfathers, and even our mothers and fathers—all of those who were denied their authentic paths.

Before journeying with this practice, I struggled with a guilt that would haunt me in moments of rest and self-care. Since my twenties, I'd tried to take care of myself but was never really consistent with it. Something always came up, and someone always needed me first. By the time I had time for myself, I was too tired or felt obligated to finish up more chores, work more, and so on. Even when I spent time with my kids unwinding watching TV, I would feel guilty for not playing a board game, doing arts and crafts, or throwing the ball around. Ugh. It was a constant narrative that I could not shut off.

This guilt came in many forms, the old language of supremacy raising its head to taunt me: I'm not doing enough, I'm not good enough, I'm not pretty enough, smart enough, funny enough, strong enough, sexy enough, Indigenous enough, Latina enough. I could be a better sister, aunt, mother, daughter, wife, and friend. Supremacy requires that you reign supreme in all things, and if you don't, then you're losing the game. And that shit ran my fucking life.

I grew up watching my parents struggle from the moment they stepped foot in this country. Immigrants are the hardest-working people yet are the ones who suffer the most. I learned that to survive, we needed to hustle. And even with hard work and perseverance, life would still throw curveballs, so we had to stay on top of our game. I was taught that there was no time for rest, no time for playing around. I learned that I was supposed to serve and take care of my family before I took care of myself. Money was for paying bills and food, not for self-care and spa days. What the hell was a spa day?

And when we did "indulge," it was a whole-family event; we didn't do it alone. We did it with parents, children, cousins, tias and tios, abuelitas and abuelos. Time for yourself was not something that existed unless it was you hiding in the bathroom, spread out on the floor, crying in your hands. Did I mention that I am the oldest of five? And we all shared a room? Oh, yeah. I had no me time until I was homeless. Even then, the guilt followed me.

This guilt was passed down by generations, and then to top it off, there was the ancestral pain and trauma. I mean, how? How do we even manage to deal with all of it? Well, we start with decolonizing our spirituality and shifting our energy and focus into the self—one day at a time, hermana, one step at a time.

## Presence Mini Ritual

To start, I want to share a mini ritual with you that will help you call yourself back to the present moment. So, if you find yourself distracted, feeling anxious, or losing interest, acknowledge this as your "ego" inner critic trying to keep you from focusing on the work, and instead of giving in, show up! Show up for yourself in those sneaky moments of self-sabotage.

As soon as you acknowledge this sneaky sabotage, take a deep breath and close your eyes. Then raise your arms, palms to the sky, and say, "I call myself back, I call myself back home, I call myself back home where I am safe and protected." Then bring your hands to your heart space and slowly take a deep breath.

Repeat one to two times or as often as needed. When I first started, I was calling my ass back home multiple times a day. Like, I really didn't like being present with myself. And that was one of the hardest things to observe. Don't confuse being alone for being present because they are not the same thing. I love being alone, but when I was alone when I first started trying to better myself and trying to get to know myself better, I would suddenly grab for my phone, get up and do random things, or check my emails for the tenth time. Once, I even decided to organize my closet, which I had not done in a few months, but when I tried to focus on getting into the work, my fight-or-flight response would kick in.

Watch yourself. Ask your Divine Self for help in observing your behaviors. You don't have to judge yourself. Stepping outside of the box or your comfort zone is hard work, and, look, we all struggle with focusing when the work is hard. But now isn't the time to ignore what you really need. Now is the time to connect into the Divine Self and start learning how to worship who you are, in all your forms.

# Self-Compassion, Mindfulness, and Self-Acceptance

I t is so easy for me to show compassion to others. In fact, I am probably the most compassionate person I know, yet when it comes to showing compassion for myself, I miss the mark. But failing to show up for yourself is a reflection of how you feel about your self-worth. And most of the time, this feeling is rooted deep in your upbringing, experiences, and past relationships—and, for some, your current relationships as well.

Sound familiar? I know, bestie, no te preocupes (don't worry), we got this!

Self-compassion is having the capacity to show up for yourself and comfort yourself with the embrace of love, encouragement, and understanding during challenging times. Self-compassion can be learned by being mindful of how we show compassion to those we love and turning it inward by learning simple techniques that bring awareness to the very act of being compassionate. Therein lies the importance of involving mindfulness with self-compassion to reach self-acceptance.

Mindfulness requires us to pay attention to any experience or emotion—positive, negative, or neutral. The mind is present and aware of what's happening within and around you, while not being judgmental, reactive, or overwhelmed. When our mind loses touch with our body and ignores the Divine Self, we become engrossed in obsessive thoughts provided by the inner critic.

Self-worship is revolutionary because when you practice it, you find yourself stripped from all the things that weigh you down. In this rise of truth, it awakens your purpose, your dreams, and your self-worth, and, most importantly, it sets you free. Like most people, self-care was not my priority because it simply wasn't something I thought I needed or deserved. I did not understand self-care outside of what the media shows us. I wasn't in the mood or in the physical state to stand on my head and try to balance my thick Cuban legs in the air while gravity laughed at me. Even with following plus-sized yogis who inspired the fuck out of me, I just didn't have the mental capacity to believe that I was capable.

I was tired, wasted, and drowning in the rivers of my past, going against the current instead of realizing that I could, at any time, stop, be still, and allow the waters to carry me forward. Self-care is the end of you resisting yourself.

Don't worry, bestie; there are ways to surrender by strengthening your self-compassion, cultivating self-acceptance, and being mindful. Get yourself a notebook to assist you through this work. Take it one day at a time.

## How to Practice Mindful Self-Compassion

Your inner critic, and the negative thoughts or emotions that control your mind, is often ingrained and hard to overcome. Developing a mindful self-compassion practice takes time and patience, and yes, bestie, a lot of compassion. Being mindful will help you develop an awareness of triggers. In addition, practicing daily mindfulness while incorporating compassion will help you pinpoint your negative emotions or thoughts, finding the source of that inner critic's voice.

### Ask Questions

To build your awareness and understanding of those judgmental, harmful, and toxic thoughts, we need to trace their roots and causes. One way to do this is to reflect on those negative emotions, ideas, and beliefs. First, make a list of the things that you think about yourself that aren't very nice. Then, for each one of them, ask yourself the following questions:

○ How does this make you feel? Be specific, and be honest.
○ Where can you trace this belief too? When did it first develop? What experience is connected to it?
○ What situations or experiences trigger this belief?
○ Does this belief belong to you? Are you ready to release it?

Next, for each thing on the list, repeat this statement: "[insert the belief here] is not my belief. It does not belong to me, and I no longer want to hold it within me. I *am* [insert a positive belief here]." For example: "That I am not good enough is not my belief. It does not belong to me, and I no longer want to hold it within me. I *am* good enough."

*Tip:* I recommend doing this exercise while recording yourself. Sit in front of your camera, and start to record after you have created the list. Then read the things on the list one at a time, and after each one, ask the questions above while looking into the camera. This recording is just for you. You can review it immediately after and reflect on it—journal on what you felt while watching it and write about any observations. I started to do this in my practice, and it helped me connect to my humanness and better understand the complexities of who I am. Reviewing the footage—and seeing myself as the vulnerable, Divine Spirit I am—was a leading factor in developing more self-compassion.

# Journal Prompts

1. How did you feel watching yourself as you spoke from the heart of your being? What emotions came up as you watched?
2. What would you say to this person? What advice would you give her?

3. Do you recognize yourself? Write down some positive things about yourself that you never noticed before.

4. What revelations, messages, or epiphanies did this bring you?

•

## Talk Back

When your self-critic starts to talk, take a moment to become aware of it. Notice the feelings and tone of voice that come with what is being said. Then begin to talk back to that inner critic. The best way to respond is with compassion. Trust me, I know it won't be easy to do this; I sometimes want to curse mine the fuck out, but we can't heal with the same essence that is making us sick. Tell the voice that you are listening and aware of its presence and that you understand that it may be worried or scared at the moment. Then allow your compassionate self to talk. Here are some things you can say: "Hey, friend, I know you didn't mean to be mean to me. Maybe you thought it might feel good because that's what you're used to saying to me, but instead, you're not feeling too good about it. And honestly, I don't feel so good about it either. So let's try being nicer for a change, and I promise you it will feel good not only to you but also to me, bestie."

Respond like you are giving a good friend advice. Keep a compassionate and gentle, loving tone. Become your own best friend. It dawned on me that through my entire life, I was primarily alone, and it was hard to make friends. But I always had me, so making myself my own BFF made sense and comforted me. It works just as if you were giving someone else love and understanding. Instead, you are directing the compassion to yourself.

*Tip*: I often do some form of physical touch during or after speaking—I give myself a hug, stroke my heart space, or gently grab my face.

I will tell you now that sometimes this work might seem silly or like it's a waste of time, but give it a chance. Be patient with the practice. It will take some time, but eventually, it will feel authentic, and it will create real change and shifts. Avoid wanting instant gratification. Just because you don't see it all instantly manifesting doesn't mean there isn't anything shifting behind the scenes. Be patient and be faithful. You are worthy of showing yourself compassion and understanding. Acknowledge and recognize that you are human. It is time to accept yourself, your whole self. #proudofyou

## Radical Self-Honesty

Radical self-honesty is about living and breathing your truth 100 percent. When we are dishonest with ourselves, we only choose to see what we want to see and believe, ignoring what we don't and creating a delusion of the self. Not surprisingly, self-honesty is a vital part of personal and spiritual growth and a key to connecting with the Divine.

The truth is that you can't hide from your own truths. Eventually, they catch up with you and can be extremely unhealthy and destructive in the long run. Being honest with ourselves can sometimes be scary and even painful. But it's necessary for our liberation, unchaining us from what's keeping us from spiritually evolving and overcoming delusional thinking about ourselves.

In my experience, being radically honest with myself caused chaos. I felt like I didn't even know who I was anymore, leaving me with a gaping hole in my soul. Or so I thought. Today I see it differently. There has never been a hole in my soul because my soul is Divinely whole.

Being radically self-honest asks that you:

- ○ admit to yourself how you truly feel
- ○ accept only what feels aligned to you and decline what does not
- ○ admit when you are wrong, make a mistake, or fuck up
- ○ admit when you need to rest, recover, and recuperate
- ○ check yourself on your own bullshit, foolishness, and ignorance
- ○ take time to uncover your true desires, dreams, and goals
- ○ admit how certain people really make you feel
- ○ face your flaws, weaknesses, and bad habits
- ○ admit when you need help from others or professional help, like

therapy (Though being able to afford therapy is a privilege not many people have, check my sources section through the QR code, BFF, for the hookup!)

Self-honesty doesn't necessarily ask that you open up to others about things you were dishonest about, even though there are definitely situations where I recommend it, especially if the person in question is your partner, good friend, or a close family member you trust and you feel like it will bring you both some healing. Do as much as you can and take your time—one day at a time, BFF.

## WHERE TO START

Start with compassion. It is your best tool in helping you through this journey—that and patience. Once you start to become honest with yourself, you will discover the magic in radical self-honesty. Things will begin to align, and the more you do it, the more intuitive the process becomes, connecting you deeper into healing and into your Divine Self. A few months into this practice, it will become second nature to tap into the observer role, watching your life through the perspective of radical self-honesty and deep self-truth.

Remember, we are not aiming for perfection, and I do not expect myself or you to become an expert observer. But when you put effort and intention into your practices, you can imagine the radical changes and spiritual growth that will happen. This is a lifelong journey, bestie, and you might as well implement moments of magic along the way, which starts with letting go of instant gratification and expectations. Here are some ways to practice self-honesty:

## PAY ATTENTION TO YOUR EMOTIONS

Emotions can be complicated. It's easy to find the root cause of some emotions, but others are just mindless creatures that like to haunt us for no apparent reason. Yet even those still have a purpose; they might just be harder to find.

Have you ever wanted to go to a real-life magic school? Well, guess what? *Life* is a real-life magic school, and you are the ritual through which you can manifest the future you desire. The ingredients are the things we allow within us, and if we allow ingredients that don't align with what we wish to manifest, then we boil over. We must be willing to remove the ingredients that do not serve the purpose we wish to accomplish.

Emotions are powerful guides that can lead us deeper into who we are. I personally get excited now when some random emotion shows up trying to cause trouble. I'm like, "Hey there, you must be lost, let's take care of that." Even though sometimes I really want to say, "Who do you think you are showing up unannounced?" But I hold myself responsible for these emotions and approach them the way I would want to be treated if I were lost. And honestly, I've become more compassionate along the way.

Emotions can be detrimental to your life and self-goals; they can lead you toward or away from the magic that lives within us all.

To stand in your magic, you have to face your emotions.

Start right away, right now, in fact. What is happening in your head? Your body? What are your emotions trying to say?

For me right now, there is an anxiety that keeps banging her head into my bones. What a bitch, right? But where did she come from? I've felt her a few times while writing this book, and she seems to want me to crumble and fall into a ball of fear. Looking deeper, she comes from the root of me thinking I am not good enough to write this book. Because when I really listen in and tune in to her frequency, I hear her saying, "You are nobody," "You aren't relatable," "Who are you to write this book?"

But luckily, I have my homegirl, Divine Self, who puts her hand on my shoulder and sits me the fuck back down so I can get to writing. It's a struggle, best friend, and it won't always be easy. But you will build a strong foundation on self-love, trust, worth, and faith in Spirit to help you combat the little bitches that try to pry you away from your truth.

## ACKNOWLEDGE REAL LIFE

"Fake it until you make it"? That idea is toxic, period. Don't be fake; instead, be honest about real-life circumstances and situations and work through them. Cultivate a mindset of radical acceptance, and you won't ever have to fake anything again. We do more harm by ignoring the "bad" aspects of our lives, thinking that they will magically disappear if we look the other way. But instead, they lurk behind our backs, waiting to catch up to us. I don't know about you, but I don't like anything chasing me—especially problems. Turn around, bestie; you'll be surprised at what you can get through and accomplish when you face things and learn to navigate through, rather than around, life.

## REFLECT

Reflection is a powerful tool. From scanning your day to addressing lingering things, reflection helps us understand our lives and the lives of those around us. If we don't reflect, our minds will try to make sense of life in their own way, causing more noise in our heads. These are the thoughts that keep us up at night, the truths we've refused to identify or failed to give voice to—the old "I should have said this" or "I should have done that." They stop us from getting into a deep sleep, which is where all the magic happens in the dream world. Give yourself time to reflect. Set aside some time to journal. I like to use a tape recorder as well, especially if I'm not feeling up to writing.

Reflection is vital in being able to master the Divine Self. Once your day is over, unwind, make yourself a cup of tea, wear your comfy pj's, and spend ten to fifteen minutes a day with your journal. Here are some things you can ask yourself:

○ How am I feeling? What emotions are present?
○ How does my body feel today? Why do I think that is?
○ How did things go today?
○ What can I celebrate? (Remember, celebrate the small wins and accomplishments as well as the big ones.)

- What could I have done better?
- Who pissed me off today? Why do I think that is? What am I going to do about it?
- What am I grateful for today?
- Who's the baddest bitch that ever lived? (Mm-hmm, that's right. You, bestie!)

Cut off all the distractions—TV, music, social media, and so on. This is *your* time with yourself and your mind. Be honest, be compassionate, and, most importantly, be real with yourself. When we give ourselves time to reflect, we learn more about ourselves and our patterns, and we receive greater insight and wisdom for the days ahead by understanding the day that just passed.

## ADMIT WHEN YOU MAKE MISTAKES

Admit it, hija, you forgot to take out the chicken again! Ugh, I don't know why time after time I forget to take the damn chicken out to defrost. My mother stopped asking me after a while and passed down the responsibility to one of my sisters #sorrykathy. Maybe it's because my sun is in Pisces, my moon in Cancer, and my rising in Libra. Eighty percent of the time, I am daydreaming. But admitting our mistakes is the cornerstone of growth, so I have promised myself to always suck it up and admit when I am wrong or make mistakes. This has also tremendously strengthened my relationship with my partner, and it has helped me become more honest and comfortable in my skin.

It's hard admitting when we are wrong, and it's definitely not fun. But avoiding responsibility isn't a cute look, honie; it's not cute at all. Protecting the ego with excuses or blaming others will not fix the fact that you made a mistake. If you keep telling yourself that you aren't capable of handling lessons, guess what the universe will keep bringing you? Mm-hmm, more lessons and probably some of the very same things you keep ignoring or not admitting to. Only a person who admits their mistakes can learn from them, correct them, and move on.

Honesty takes practice, and it is something we need to practice daily. It takes a lot of self-awareness, which won't come right away; it will take some time to trust the process. But trust me when I say that it changes everything. When self-honesty is implemented in your practice, there is no telling how powerful it will be in your spiritual growth. Take a deep breath, bestie. We are in it now.

## The Call for a Deeper Commitment

How many times have you started to do something and then not followed through? Tasks, projects, diets, courses, programs, books. How about self-care? I'm looking you dead in the eyes (insert glaring emoji here). Self-honesty, remember? It's okay; we are all guilty of this in one way or another. And this is why self-care is part of this practice.

This is also why you made the agreement at the start of this book, an agreement that you vowed to. We don't want this to be another empty promise, another false start that you attempt for a few days but then abandon because it's gotten hard or boring or you can't quite fit it into your schedule. Having self-accountability means you're fully responsible for your choices and actions. When you are self-accountable, you are taking responsibility for your well-being, which means you are also holding yourself accountable for caring for your mind, body, and Spirit. All new habits and behaviors start with motivation and willingness, but accountability is the way in which you accomplish and follow through. And beyond setting your goals, it also means you can call yourself out when you're unable to do what you said you would.

"It's not always possible to be your best self. Sometimes you make mistakes. And sometimes you break promises that you made to yourself."

—Nedra Glover Tawwab

How are you going to uplevel your life if you aren't holding yourself accountable? Listen, I'll be the first to admit that self-accountability was not my strong suit before this practice, but I began to shift my perspective when I started to notice that in not following through, the only one I was hurting was myself. In my case, not holding myself accountable was another form of self-sabotage. And all it did was hold me back from my big aspirations, goals, and dreams. By keeping yourself accountable, you are helping yourself to follow through, and by following through, you are closer to your desired outcomes.

In order to be accountable, you need to create clarity and intention. You must be clear about why you are doing the work, and you must plan out where you want it to take you. This is especially important in self-care because it creates intention and purpose in what you want to do or accomplish. Why are you brushing your teeth? Why are you putting on that mud mask? Why are you exercising? Why are you eating healthier? Have a super-clear *why* and a clear vision of what that journey looks like and what the best way is to get there.

Think about your goals and priorities in life and make a list. Then review each one and ask yourself the *why*, and then plan out the *how*. This will help you overcome roadblocks, reminding you of the intentions behind everything you do.

And then carve out time in your calendar for the *how*'s.

For example, I plan out one to two months of self-care at a time, and I include taking days off to rest and recuperate. I set appointments and plan for the spa, nails, checkups, nature hikes, rest, family time, and girl time, and I even put in tiny rituals I can do myself, like massaging my own feet and soaking them, reminding myself to take supplements, making time for reading, meditation, breathwork, exercise, and baths, and even giving myself mini face massages. But the most crucial self-care planning I do is not planning too much at one time. I learned that to start a routine and successfully keep accountability with it, you should not overwhelm yourself. Keep it simple at first as you begin to cultivate more time for and with yourself.

*Self-worship is a ritualistic practice that takes you on
a journey to remembering who you are. The more you practice,
the more dangerous you become to the things and people
that try to bring you down.*

## 7

### DEVOTIONAL

# Building a Healthy Relationship with Self

You are the one constant in your life and journey. Your relationship with yourself is vital in your spiritual growth, your well-being, and living your Divined life. We aren't taught how to build relationship skills with ourselves, and in my opinion, it should be one of the first things we learn how to do.

Let's start now. Do you want to craft a relationship with yourself that is positive and supportive? One that provides you with everything you need, allowing others to be added blessings but not the source of your wholeness? Because I can promise you, no one—not your partner, your parents, even your children—can make you whole but you.

In life's journey, we carry a constant companion, that inner voice inside our heads. But for many of us, the relationship between ourselves and that voice isn't so positive. In fact, it can be downright toxic. Now, just to clarify, this voice is not from our Divine Self. Your Divine Self is love and will always support you, cheer you on, and have your back. Even when trying to send you a warning, the warning comes without fear; it's more of a knowing. The other voice is what some call the ego, but I believe it is actually programming from the past—a broken record from your childhood, your parent's childhood, the centuries stretching out behind you.

We don't want to respond by being mean or dismissing it. We want to acknowledge its presence, discover the root cause of it, and begin to heal it. Self-criticism is not something to overlook, and it is definitely not something you heal through spiritual bypassing. It will still be there, and it will worsen by ignoring its existence.

As we begin to build a healthier relationship with ourselves, we must create new rules and rituals on which to build self-respect, self-confidence, and self-love that's not rooted in the standards of the capitalist colonial system but in our great Divinity and innate power.

To begin, we need to start with boundaries. Setting boundaries wasn't something I ever thought I needed to do; in fact, when it started to become something people talked about, I thought, Eh, I don't need to do that, I'm good. Then my friends began to send me their boundaries lists, and I thought, WTF is this? Everyone was suddenly setting boundaries, and I felt taken aback; honestly, it was a little triggering. And because of that observation, I thought, Why is this triggering me? Why am I not interested in setting boundaries?

Well, first off, I had no idea what a healthy boundary really looked like. I never had boundaries growing up; they were nonexistent. My family of seven lived in a small apartment, and I shared a room with my four sisters. We all ate whatever was given to us, and we had to eat it even if we didn't like it. Opinions weren't welcomed. Everyone had access to all my belongings, and our bedroom door was never to be closed. Then I was homeless for a while, so I never had a solid place or space that I knew was mine, and by the time I got back on my feet, I had roommates, and then I became a mother and a wife. I never had the chance to establish boundaries, ever.

This subject is a hefty one. I could write an entire book on setting boundaries, but someone amazing already did that—I recommend following Nedra Glover Tawwab on social media. She wrote the book *Set Boundaries, Find Peace*. She shares so much information on her accounts that I know it will help you in your journey with setting boundaries with others. I also share her details and links in the resource section.

In 2019, the more I learned about the importance of having boundaries, the more I started to set them. By the time 2020 came around, it became my favorite thing to do. I even started to look at it from an internal perspective, thinking about what it meant to set boundaries with myself and not just with others. I found a lack of information on this, so I began to focus on expanding with it. What I found was that by setting boundaries with myself, I began to create a truer and more powerful bond with myself.

A boundary is a limit or space between you and another person. This isn't an obvious line others can see, so communicating with them is how they will know what your boundaries are. The same is true with yourself. Setting healthy boundaries with myself helped me establish my identity, and it was an essential aspect of my mental health as well.

After diving deeper into this form of setting boundaries, I found that I became more confident and started to trust myself more. That's a heavy phrase, *trust myself more*. What I mean is that I didn't trust myself before, and that was a heartbreaking realization. Though I had trust issues in general, I could not even trust myself to consistently do the things I needed to better my health, relationships, and life. Because I practice self-honesty and compassion for the self, I approached this with love and understanding.

Setting boundaries with yourself is also a powerful form of self-care. Remember, you are responsible for your own well-being; setting boundaries is the bridge that connects the *why* and the *how* to make sure you follow your desired path.

*She remembered who she was, and without mercy, she destroyed everything that ever made her feel like she wasn't whole.*

I'm the boss when it comes to planning, creating, and mapping out everything to the last detail, but inconsistency was my dark truth, and I had to own that shit. This is why after leaving social media, I decided to shut everything down—my brand, business, and services—all so I could strip down to nothing and find myself there. I knew that if I was able to build up solid boundaries in every space of my life, I could start to rebuild more solid foundations for honoring the intentions and goals I had for my work, health, and life. I'm aware it was a privilege to be able to do this with the support of the book profits I had saved. Not everyone can or has to take it to such extremes, but we all can shut down certain aspects of our lives—including our relationships with food, sex, drugs, alcohol, work, family, friends, or social media. We can build powerful boundaries as we create the space we need to breathe and self-worship.

When you set a boundary with yourself, you're saying, "Here's the line I can't cross." For me, it was a way to re-parent myself. It gave me a sense of honor, security, safety, and structure that I didn't have as a child. Many of us had parents who did not have boundaries themselves, so we never learned how to create them. Raise a finger for each one that applies:

- ○ One or both parents did not keep promises.
- ○ One or both parents drank excessively.
- ○ One or both parents smoked excessively.
- ○ One or both parents never saved money and spent it recklessly.
- ○ One or both parents didn't have time to listen to you.
- ○ Your parents didn't set healthy limits for themselves.
- ○ One or both parents didn't have rules, had inconsistent rules, or had extremely strict rules.

All seven fingers up? Take a deep breath, bestie. We are not here to shame our parents. Divinity knows they have gone through their own struggles and did not have the privilege of taking more time for themselves. If either of them was working to keep a roof over your head, then they probably didn't have time to spare, let alone set boundaries and indulge in self-care. However, we are not dismissing that it had an impact on your upbringing. #wehaveworktodo

It's important to note that setting boundaries may be harder for those who have some mental health problems or addictions that can impair their thinking or make it extremely hard to monitor and set limits. If this relates to you, consider getting support from a friend or family member who can help you stay consistent with your boundaries. Again, seeing a therapist in this case is also a helpful avenue to take. See the sources for options for those that need financial assistance.

## How to Set Boundaries with Yourself

First, you have to identify areas of your life that need limits, structure, and account-ability. These usually are your priorities, values, and goals you want to see through, such as finances, mental health, emotional well-being, physical wellness, nutrition, and so forth. Remember to practice self-honesty and self-compassion while establishing self-boundaries. And don't try to set too many boundaries all at once. Here are some examples of boundaries for your spiritual, physical, and emotional well-being. Take the ones that relate to you and apply them, and, of course, create your own:

- ○ I will not deny myself rest.
- ○ I will stop questioning my worth.
- ○ My well-being is more important than being "productive."
- ○ I will stop minimizing my achievements.
- ○ I will not overwhelm myself by overloading my schedule.
- ○ I will no longer give my energy freely; energy is sacred currency.
- ○ I will not allow someone else to tell me what my liberation, self-care, and rest looks like or should be.
- ○ I will no longer worry or stress about people who don't give a fuck about me.
- ○ I will stop playing small and take up space.
- ○ I will pay attention to my emotions and stop downplaying them.
- ○ I will speak up when I feel disrespected or hurt.
- ○ I will not suppress my feelings anymore. I will allow myself to cry when I want to.

My boundaries may not look like your boundaries. We all have different priorities and things that we need to set boundaries around. The boundaries you create for yourself should reflect your needs and priorities, but I'm sharing some of mine to give you an idea of what boundaries or limits can look like:

- Shop locally before shopping online.
- Make sure to support BBIPOC businesses.
- Stick to my budget; no overspending.
- A few times a week, try to listen to empowering, healing, or inspirational artists/songs.
- Keep screens (television, phone, technology) out of my bedroom.
- Stop working, accepting text messages, checking emails, and checking social media after 5:00 p.m. Create time for family and myself.
- Do not answer work-related emails on the weekends.
- Never skip my morning- or night-routine rituals.
- Don't question my journey. Trust in Divinity and self.
- Read a book or listen to a podcast if I am bored instead of going on social media.
- Avoid added sugar until I get my health back in check.
- Have sex or masturbate seven times a week. (LOL, joking, bestie—I *wish*! One to two times a week, at a minimum.)
- Always tend to my Altar, no excuses.
- Prioritize self-care before anything or anyone else, unless there is an emergency.
- Make more time for people who are like-minded and aspire to live their Divined lives.
- Avoid people who drain my energy or stress me out, etc.
- Cut a conversation short if I feel uncomfortable or if the person is vomiting their emotional baggage on me.
- Don't start a new project before completing the one I am on.
- Don't agree to join, sign something, or say yes until I've slept on it.
- Stop giving my time to people who troll my social media and to people who hate on me #deleteblockbitches (insert tongue emoji here).

When we begin to acknowledge the Altar within, we weave ourselves into a sacred invitation with everything around us, welcoming us home.

May you come to see that you are on purpose for a purpose. There is no mistake in your miraculous presence. There is no question in the Divine part you play in the world. From the moment you wake and even into your dreams, you are ritualistically participating in Ceremony. Your breath is a ritual, your tongue is a ritual, your movements are rituals, your heart beating is a ritual; all of you is beautifully magical and sacred. Many of us have forgotten the sacred element of Divinity in all of life. We are consumed by technology, worshipping our gadgets and toys rather than the remembrance of our Divine existence.

*I am capable and worthy of setting boundaries and honoring them. I am responsible for my mental, physical, emotional, and spiritual well-being. I will practice self-compassion and honesty and remind myself that I am doing all that I can and that that is more than enough.*

## 8

**DEVOTIONAL**

# Acknowledge
# the Altar Within

E ight months off social media really does open your eyes to the world
around and within you. The more time and space I created by being liberated from my phone, the more I was able to take note of everything
I did and why. I re-awoke to this feeling of belonging I hadn't felt in a
long time—belonging to the enchanting rhythm and flow of life, the seasons, the
moon phases, the stars and planets, the waters, the Earth, the animals, and the
sky. My body, mind, and Spirit were intertwined with all that is. Life started to feel
more like what my grandmothers would say about it, "La vida está conectada,
una con el aliento de la Diosa," meaning life is all connected, we are one with the
breath of the Goddess.

I understood what they were saying but had never really lived it until after I
started this practice. Life became the world you see in the *Avatar* movie, the world
I would see when in Ceremony with my tribe and elders, the world I see when I
take my ancestral sacred medicine—making even the ordinary things more meaningful and full of intention and purpose, elevating them into a ritual.

You can lift your everyday actions and routines into the realm of Ceremony,
turning them into an act of ritualistic devotion. Even when I'm having a tough day,
I do my best to stay in Ceremony and connect into ritual throughout my day. It's
the intention behind your actions that matters. Spirit sees and knows all; you are
seen, bestie.

Routines are repetitive actions that are done daily or regularly. With routines, you are accomplishing a task or goal; there is no real essence of purpose other than it has to be done. For example, when I looked at the act of brushing my teeth, I asked myself, "Why do I brush my teeth?" And my answer was "To avoid bad breath and have healthy teeth." Just by recognizing the intention behind the action, I turned the routine into a ritual, creating something more meaningful. Now, I brush my teeth because they are part of my temple, and by taking care of my teeth, I am honoring and respecting my body. #heartblown

Do you see? It's a mind shift, a new perspective. Rituals carry meaningful intentions that turn your life into a Ceremony. The essence of living life as a Ceremony is to go inward and transcend, to bring yourself back home to the Divine Self. It is guiding your mind to be still and present, expanding your Spirit, and plugging into Divinity.

Even rest can be an act of ritual when you integrate an intention with it. For example, "I am resting because I am worthy of recuperating and healing." It now has a purpose that's sacred and so it becomes a ritual. Rituals can be small or extravagant, they can be complex or simple, but the one constant is the purpose you give to those actions.

Not all things in your day-to-day routine hold a meaningful purpose that will make them feel like a ritual. Scrolling through social media mindlessly, checking your mail, surfing the internet, watching TV, and, depending on your job, spending time at work might be challenging to ritualize. And that's okay; magic is found in the pockets of calm and centering you find throughout your day, becoming the salve that soothes your soul and enhances your life. Even in those mundane tasks you may find purpose and intention with which you can align, making them more personal and purposeful. The key is to avoid doing things mindlessly and without any real intention behind them. Start with your morning and then work your way down the rest of the day. Try not to drive yourself crazy by focusing on everything you do at once; section your days off and start with one section at a time. Eventually, life will start to feel a lot more joyful than it may have felt in the past.

Time used to get away from me. It was like I was constantly fighting against the clock. I don't know about you, but that scared the shit out of me, the feeling of my days just passing by, twirling all around me as I tried to catch up. Now that I've practiced living in Ceremony and becoming the ritual of my life, everything is a symphony orchestrated by me. Even when the world is moving quickly around me, I am still.

Life moves fast when you have days packed with routine and no real sense of being present. One of the most significant benefits of living a life in Ceremony and creating these rituals is that you slow down life; you become one with the movement of life. You become one with the breath of Divinity.

67

## Turning Routine into Ritual

Create a list of things you do from the start of your day until you go to bed. Like I mentioned, start by sectioning off your day and working through one section at a time—for example, morning, noon, evening, and night. Work on one section for a week or so and then move on to the next. If you need more time for each section, take it! Remember, this book is a practice for *you*, a practice that is meant to fit *your* lifestyle. There is no right way or wrong way. You do what feels right, bestie. As you move through the different activities and parts of your day, ask yourself:

○ Why do I do this?
○ Who am I doing this for?
○ Does it align with my needs and desires?
○ Why is it important to me?
○ What is the purpose of this?
○ Where will it get me, or what will it accomplish?
○ How can I make this more intentional?
○ How can I make this more purposeful?

Let's go over some examples of a few daily routines you're probably already doing, and let's add a bit of intention behind them and shift them into ritual:

○ **Showering:** Bathing is an ancient sacred ritual. Water is life, water is healing, and water is cleansing to the Spirit, not just the body. I *love* my showers and baths and find they are the most ritualistic moments in my day-to-day life. To help turn your bathing into a ritual, remind yourself of what a privilege it is to have running water when many people in many parts of the world do not. Before I get into the shower or bath, I thank the Water Spirit. I get on my knees and say a little prayer of gratitude and thankfulness. While bathing, I calm my mind from the outside noise, turning inward as the waters rush over my flesh. It's an active meditation experience.

Many people experience creativity bursts while bathing, and others experience connection with Spirit. Whether you experience either of those or not, just the intention of being grateful is powerful. Be mindful as you lather, wash your hair, and so on. Be present with yourself and your body. Envision the waters clearing away tension, stress, and worries. Envision them resetting your Aura and cleansing your Spirit. You don't have to take long. I know most of you have to get to work and have other things to do, but do your best to make it intentional in your own way, and you will see how powerful a simple act can become.

○ **Self-Care:** It may seem silly to think that self-care wouldn't be considered a ritual, but often self-care is done without intention. For example, we might get a facial, go to yoga, head to the gym, lather on lotion, or choose a healthier meal, but these things are often just done with no actual thought going into them, or they might be performed for a superficial reason rather than an intentional and purposeful one. This is not true for everyone, but let's see how we can add more intention to self-care. First, ask yourself the *why* and get a little more intimate with the purpose of these acts.

For example, instead of, "I am putting on this mud mask because my favorite influencer uses it and says it's great for her skin," you might say, "I am putting on this mud mask to show myself love and care, as the ingredients reconnect me to the Earth." The difference lies in making it personal, intimate, and purposeful. Many times, people don't look at what's in the products they use or learn about the cultures and origins behind the activities they do—like yoga or lighting herbs to cleanse your home. Get intimate with the things you do and learn more about them, again asking *why* and connecting to them in a deeper and more meaningful way.

○ **Cooking:** My favorite thing in the whole world aside from plants and my garden is cooking. Cooking is magical! It is ritualistic and makes me feel in tune with my ancestors. I am reminded of my mother when I'm in the kitchen, which brings a lot of healing to my Spirit. I sat and watched my mother cook as a baby and throughout my childhood. I mentioned in my first book, *Witchery*, that my mother is a Kitchen Witch, and her most powerful magic can be seen and felt in her presence while in the kitchen. Food is rooted in culture and connected to our ancestors. Therefore it should be ritualized with intention and purpose. Gathering your ingredients and knowing why they are essential for a particular meal, and working with the Fire Spirit to create a manifestation of love, medicine, and magic that nourishes your body is, in my opinion, a spell. To make cooking a ritual, be present and observe your flow with the Spirits of the ingredients, the fire, and the ancestors whispering to your soul. Even if you aren't any good at it, you can still be mindful and thankful for the food you have created and are eating. Most importantly, be proud of your accomplishment; focus on progress, not perfection.

I know many of you may not have the time to cook daily, but try at least once or twice a week if you can. Go on YouTube for millions of free recipes if you don't have recipes passed down from family. I have tons of recipes from my family, but I still look up recipes from my culture and give them a go. Connect with your parents and ask them to teach you how to make your favorite meals. If you are lucky enough to have grandparents that are still alive, ask them as well. It is truly a beautiful bonding experience and will make the act of cooking your own meals that much more purposeful.

Living life as a Ceremony can manifest enchantment in your life—a deeper meaning to life, a sense of purpose, and a connectedness that we all desire.

## Powerful Morning Rituals and Practices

No one but you can say what constitutes the perfect morning rituals and practices for you. We are all different and have different lives, situations, beliefs, needs, and wants. This is why I do not outline a one-way morning routine but instead offer a list of rituals and practices you can look through to see what connects and works best for you—an inspiration list, if you will. If you long for more meaning and purpose in your life, you might try some of these ideas; morning practices full of meaningful rituals can give you just that. They are a powerful way to get you going for the rest of the day.

My mornings used to be consumed by other people's needs and wants. Even now, I still have to navigate through being a mom to two teen boys while also making time for myself. I'm no good to them if I am not good to myself. I had to set a lot of healthy boundaries with them. You matter, bestie, and your needs and wants are just as important as those of your kids and the people you love.

Children mimic and reflect what they see and experience at home. Setting a practice for yourself is a powerful way to teach them to care and love and worship themselves. I even helped my sons create a morning ritual of their own. Every day, my heart melts as I witness them doing things that are good for their mental, physical, and spiritual well-being. Is it perfect? Heck no, but it's better than not having any ritual at all.

Just the other day, I started to journal in the morning, and one of my sons decided he wanted to be extra snippy with me before I even had a chance to brush my teeth #spirittakethewheel. But having done my practice for months now, I was able to respond more mindfully and compassionately, rather than just react. Morning rituals and practices don't have to be complicated or elaborate. They can be simple and still be powerful. Here are some ideas:

- **Be still and come back to body:** This is the very first thing I do once I wake. I give myself a chance to come back to my body. I take three deep breaths and then slowly start to wiggle my toes and fingers. I then begin to sway my body gently like a snake, side to side, waking up my temple. I then hum for about one to three minutes under my breath, taking in a deep breath before I hum. I hold the hum for as long as I can before I start the next one. This helps me call back to myself from all time and all places, giving my body the cue that I am ready to go.
- **Greet the morning:** Open up your curtains and windows. Let the sunlight and fresh air in. Greet the sun, the sky, the birds, and that little spider who keeps a web in your windowpane.
- **Pray/give thanks:** Give thanks for living another day, for being able to start a fresh new day, or for whatever you are grateful for. Express it, feel it, and charge your body with good-feel vibrations.
- **Stretch/do yoga:** Movement in the morning has been my go-to. I spend at least ten to fifteen minutes stretching my body and loosening up kinks. I'm forty; this body cracks and pops, LOL. I need this movement to help my body better sustain the coming of the day and to avoid injury.
- **Exercise:** I am a fire starter. My body is *hot*, literally like a furnace. If I do not move the energy around and release some of that heat, I start to become anxious, stressed, and scattered. Exercise, in general, is not only for looking and feeling good physically; it also helps to spiritually release lingering energetic baggage. Plus, that post-workout natural high is addictive.

○ **Journal/do a brain dump:** Dumping whatever is lingering in my mind onto the paper is so important in my practice. I do long-form journaling, where I write down stream-of-conscious thoughts to clear my mind. Go ahead and try it. Take a moment to sit, and start to write whatever comes. It may be tasks and to-do lists or it may be a song stuck in your head. It may be parts of a dream you had. Whatever it is, let it all out and give your mind the space to just be. I do this before I meditate. Which brings us to . . .

○ **Meditate/sit in silence:** Clear your mind and shut off the noise. Meditation can be done many ways. If you are new to it, try my guided meditations, which you can find in the supplemental content for this book via the QR code. Meditate or just sit in silence. It gives you a chance to check in and tap into Divinity. Meditation brings clarity, creativity, and inspiration, not to mention it is incredible for spiritual growth and your well-being.

○ **Avoid technology:** Try to avoid your phone and social media for at least the first two hours after waking. This can easily interrupt your vibes by taking you down a rabbit hole, and, before you know it, you've spent a good amount of your morning scrolling mindlessly. It took me a while, but I finally have no urge to reach for my phone to entertain me. Set hard boundaries and hold yourself accountable. I recommend doing this until you can take your power back and use it without getting engulfed.

○ **Set a daily intention:** What intention do you wish to hold space for on this particular day? Choose an intention that will guide you through the day ahead. For example, if I am visiting family that day, I make sure to set an intention of patience. Porque ouufff. Sometimes it is what saves me from losing my shit. I love my family, but it takes a lot of energy to be around them for long periods. We are a huge family with a gazillion kids. Patience. Patience. Patience. Did I mention we are Cuban? #quebulla

○ **Visualize:** Take a moment to visualize how you desire your day to go. Watch yourself as you navigate the day, observe how you encounter people, and feel into the vibrations you want to set.

○ **Do breathwork:** Breathwork is a breathing exercise that brings you inward. It is another form of meditation. Being one with the breath and the flow of your energy helps lower anxiety, stress, and worry, and it has helped me lift my Spirit, ground my body, and open myself up to receive downloads and messages from the Divine. (Again, see the QR code for a daily meditation breathwork ritual for activating the Divine Self and remembering who you are.)

○ **Read inspirational texts:** I love me some inspiring words, and the mornings are the best time to get some into your soul. It can be a book, a passage, a poem, a story, or actual inspirational quotes. I try to look for a new one each day. It solidifies my mindset and opens my heart, making me feel like I can accomplish anything—or rather, *reminding* me that I can accomplish anything.

○ **Do a self-scan:** A self-scan is one of my go-to rituals. It gives me an intimate connection with my whole self, allowing me to adjust and align. A self-scan puts you in tune with yourself, so you can see what feels off and needs your care. You can stand or sit. Then relax your body and calm your mind. Take a few deep breaths until you feel present. Close your eyes and envision a bright blue light, almost like a laser light, starting from your crown and moving to your feet. (I do it this way because ending at the feet helps ground you after you're done.) Start at the crown of your head and slowly move the light down your forehead, then down the mouth, down the neck, and so on. Make sure to go slow and observe any signals, tingling, pain, or vibrations in any one spot or space. Envision the light pulsating over it and filling it with love and healing; continue to scan and repeat three times.

○ **Say affirmations:** Saying affirmations to yourself helps to rewire your mindset, rewriting a new story that you tell yourself. However, affirmations can be difficult for those who have a more challenging time believing positive statements about themselves. Be careful that they aren't causing more harm than good. Give them a try, but if you see they are just not doing it for you, come back and try them at a later date. Remember, take your time and do what you can

○ **Listen to a podcast/audiobook:** There are so many great podcasts and audiobooks out there! My favorite places to listen are in my car, in the waiting room, while I shop for groceries, and when I take my morning walks. Feed your soul, BFF.

○ **Make yourself some tea:** The process of making tea is so magical to me. It is one of my favorite rituals and one that has helped me connect deeper with the medicine and wisdom of the herbs, flowers, and roots in my tea. When done mindfully, it can be an act of meditation as well.

○ **Worship/spend time in your sacred place:** Every morning, I tend to my Altars. I have multiple spaces because that's what works for me, my needs, and my beliefs—they allow me to reflect and honor, to show gratitude and respect. A space that reminds you of who you are and the magic you hold can be extremely powerful. This space is dedicated to you and your Spirit team, whoever they may be, and will become the place to connect to Divinity.

Your Altar or sacred space can look and feel however you desire. When I was younger and homeless, I did not have the means to keep an Altar. All I used were tea candles, rocks, stones, shells, and a cactus I purchased for a dollar at the Dollar Store. This Altar meant everything to me and was still sacred and powerful even though it wasn't extravagant. This is why I always tell people that intention is everything! You do not need to have a lot to make a worthy sacred space or Altar. You do not need to have all the tools, crystals, herbs, and candles to make it feel magical. You can make it as extravagant as you want or as simple as you want. It holds power either way.

---

# Self-Worship Altar/Space

A self-worship Altar? Yes, please! When I first began practicing self-worship, I thought, "Hmmm, what if I set up an Altar to myself? What if this Altar was dedicated to me, by me?" My self-worship Altar is now a space that reflects who I am and reminds me of my power, magic, and sacredness. I think it is necessary to worship yourself, not just because it is direct worship to the creator and your Divine Self but also because you are a true Diosa, a sacred being, a magical being, one who is worthy of praise.

Your self-worship Altar will serve as a daily reminder to take better care of yourself, honor yourself, tap into your Divine Self, and remind you that you are a #badbitch!

It will be your sacred space where you can do rituals, meditations, self-reflection, or ceremonies, to name a few ideas. You can do quite literally anything you want with it and put whatever you want on it, but I created a guide to give you some ideas of what I think a self-worship Altar or space should have. Take from it what you like and remember to do your own thing, add your own flair, and set those intentions. Spirituality and witchcraft are not one-blueprint-fits-all. They were never meant to be confined by laws and rules. They are intended to be as unique as the person who wields their power. That's you, best friend, that's you!

A self-worship Altar is an extension of you and your beliefs. It should reflect the things you love and your uniqueness. Everything you put on it should matter to you, mean something to you, and, most importantly, honor who you are.

Here are some ideas for you from the self-worship Altar I created for myself:

- a mirror (A mirror at your self-worship Altar is powerful. It will not only reflect your image and allow you to look at the being you are honoring; it is also a beautiful way to say your affirmations, prayers, and intentions to yourself.)
- your favorite selfies or photography of yourself
- pictures of places you love or that mean something to you
- your favorite poems, passages, or affirmations

- ❍ your go-to book(s) that inspire and empower you
- ❍ your favorite candle(s)
- ❍ your favorite flowers and plants
- ❍ your favorite scents, incense, or oils
- ❍ crystals that you feel connected to
- ❍ sacred pieces of jewelry—ones you love and wear often
- ❍ sacred items that represent you and your culture, beliefs, and practices
- ❍ a journal and pen
- ❍ tarot or oracle cards, or any divination tool that you love and are connected to
- ❍ your favorite perfume to spray over the Altar and on yourself
- ❍ your favorite colors
- ❍ an offering, such as your favorite cakes, chocolate, food, coffee, or cannabis. (This is your Altar, best friend, and you offer the things that you love to the Divine Self within.)

## Self-Worship Practice

Sit with yourself and have some tea, coffee, or, my favorite, cannabis. I try to sit at my self-worship Altar and look in the mirror and have a chat with myself every day, just as if I had a girlfriend over and wanted to share everything with her, from my day's accomplishments to releasing frustrations. I ask myself, What happened today? Anything exciting or new? Did you run into issues today? How did you tackle them? Offer a whole rundown of your day with your Divine Self.

If you find that you start to become negative about others or life in general, remember to reply as your Divine Self with compassion, self-honesty, and understanding. Don't judge yourself for what you share or how you share it. Be you, as you are. It may seem silly or challenging at first, but it will become so much easier. And the connection you will start to build with Spirit is *insanely* delicious.

# Energy Hygiene

Clearing your energy should be a daily hygiene ritual. It is just as important as taking a shower or brushing your teeth. We are all empaths; it is an innate gift we carry here on Earth. Many people don't even know they are empaths and struggle with the side effects of not having their energy cleansed and cleared. I especially see this cause harm in children. They are more vulnerable to the energies of others, making it harder for them to be in tune with their own selves. As an empath, you feel other people's energies and most often take them on. However, we are also impacted by the energies in everything around us, making it highly overwhelming when the world is in distress, which can be draining. If your gifts or senses are more enhanced than those of others, you especially need to think about implementing energy hygiene into your daily life.

What does it do? Well, what a shower does for your physical body, energy clearing does for your energy body. It is meant to be a sort of reset button for your Aura, clearing yourself from other people's energies that carry emotions, baggage, and often negative vibes and even bodily pains, which can fuck with your vibe, plain and simple.

Recently, I was having a conversation with a good friend, Lorriane, and we were talking about how we identify as introverts but that we also have qualities of extroverts. We realized that maybe we had it wrong all along. See, I thought I was an introvert most of my life because I did not like how I felt around people, especially the days following our time together. I would be drained, feel off, and need a vacation from people and the world. The more I thought on it though, the more I uncovered that I am not an introvert; I enjoy going out, exploring, having a good time with friends, and meeting new people. In fact, I am often the one that is most lively and interactive when out with people. It was the aftereffects that caused me to think I was an introvert.

Some side effects of being around people, going to crowded places, mindlessly scrolling through social media, or being in a toxic or harmful environment (at home or in the area where you live) are:

- irrational mood swings
- fatigue
- illness
- feeling drained of your own energy
- lack of focus or brain fog
- the inability to control your reactions or responses
- unexplained pains, emotions, anxiety, anger, stress, worry, or fear
- weakened immune system
- triggered nervous system
- feeling that your joy is depleted
- feeling that your other gifts have taken a hit (for example, your intuition may be off)

I started to think about my energy hygiene and how my elders would always warn that people like me with activated gifts needed to cleanse and clear ritually. We all do! And it is life-changing. Once you start to implement it into your practice, you will feel and see the difference.

I have many go-to rituals, but most are sacred to my ancestral practice and culture, so I am sharing some of my favorites that don't expose those practices. These are ones everyone can do for energy hygiene:

- **Take salt baths:** Salt absorbs negative energy, and when added to water and combined with herbs, crystals, and oils, the result is a powerful spiritual cleansing bath. I don't feel comfortable sharing my ancestral spiritual cleansing recipes, also known as Limpias, so I suggest doing a little research on herbs, crystals, and oils that you can use to create a cleansing bath. See the QR code for some recommendations. I recommend spending at least twenty minutes in the bath to fully submerge into the healing and cleansing properties of the water and the items you place in it.
- *Tip:* Don't have a bathtub? You can prepare a simple foot bath instead. And if you are by an ocean, waterfall, or river, bathing in Nature's waters

is the one of the best ways to clear and reset. These are my primary tools for shedding what does not belong to my energy.

○ **Unplug and find solace:** Spend some time alone; it is essential to allow your energy to take time off from others. Make sure to drink a lot of water and restorative teas, eat grounding foods, and set your space up so that it is calming. Turn your phone off or keep away from it for the day or a few hours. Unplugging from all technology helps your energy to restore and reset.

○ **Practice smoke cleansing:** Be mindful of the herbs, plants, and flowers you use to burn and cleanse with, and work with ones that are meant to clear and cleanse your energy body. Please keep in mind that people often unknowingly use herbs that do not clear the energetic body and are meant for other things. I see this *a lot* in the spiritual and witchy community because people do what they see others doing and don't truly connect to the sacred items and tools they use or take the time to find out where they come from and what their actual properties are. A lot of people post videos or pictures of themselves "clearing negative vibes" and instead are amplifying them or just moving them around. Do your research, bestie!

○ **Get some love from Mama Earth:** Being in nature is medicine for the entire self. On most days, you can find me dwelling in the embraces of our Mother. Sit under a tree, hug a tree, walk on the grass, hike a trail in the woods or mountains, swim in her sacred waters, or simply be in nature.

○ **Do breathwork:** Breathwork is fantastic for clearing and moving energy from the body. There are many sources on YouTube and breathwork teachers on social media that can help you learn how to do it. I also created some videos for you that you can access via the QR code.

79

# Shielding

I never leave the house without my shields on and activated. Although we are always protected, taking an extra step to pray to your Spirits, ancestors, and guides to keep you safe and block other people's energies from you adds an extra layer of shielding. I also create an energy shield around me, like a bubble that keeps me and my energy safely inside without the interference of the outside world.

Here's a simple way to do this:

1. Envision a golden sphere of light in front of you.
2. Walk into it.
3. Once inside, set your intentions. (For example: "This sphere is strong and protective. Nothing can get through it. I only accept loving and positive vibes to enter.")
4. Do this every day before leaving your home or right after you wake up.

We have been conditioned to live in survival mode, and this is even more true for BBIPOC. We need to give ourselves permission to self-worship without feeling guilty; we need to see how essential it is for the sustainability of our existence and for our resistance against oppression. When you are constantly told and shown that you don't matter, that your life is seen as less worthy, valid, or important, self-worship becomes a revolutionary act.

When you are constantly told what you should look like, how you should dress, how you should speak and act, and what you should do or not do, self-worship becomes a force against white imperialism. There is an activist within all our Divine Selves, and she cares for our joy, rest, health, and existence. She wants you to resist the world that seeks to change who you are, that unapologetically works in trying to strip you from your identity, truth, and sovereignty.

I am still working through this and continually reminding myself that I am worthy of self-worship and that my self-worship is my way of honoring my ancestors and Spirit. My ancestors are the reason I am here; their sacrifices and prayers are the reason I breathe today, and by living my Divined life while fighting against the systems that oppressed them and me, I am their prayers realized.

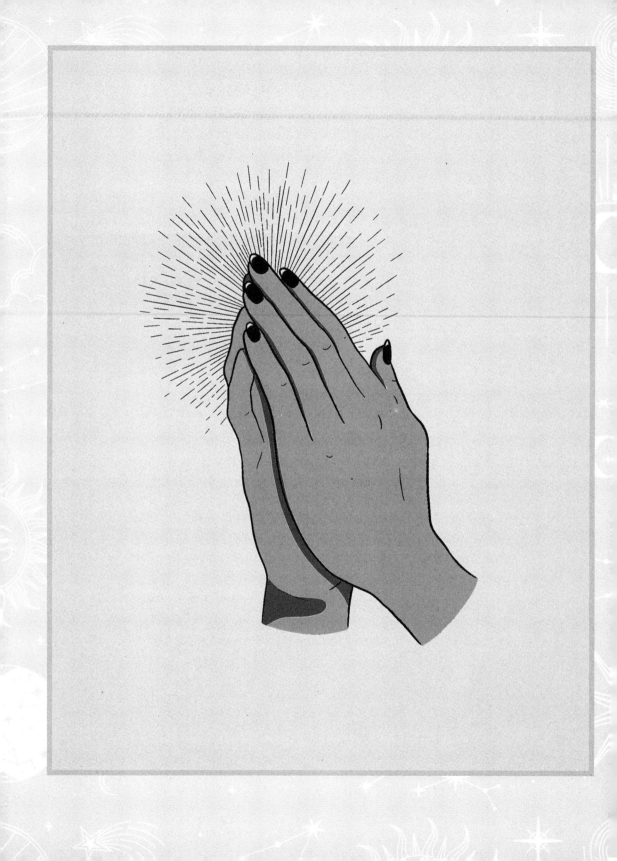

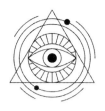

# Sacred Truths

The social justice issues in our world are incredibly overwhelming. With administrations and industries embracing white supremacy, homophobia, and transphobia (to name a few issues), it may seem like we are outnumbered and like it's almost impossible to break down these systems. Mostly this is due to how they have made us believe that they are superior and that we are no force against them. They have also managed to break us away from community, making it easier for us to not see the power that lives in unity.

Self-worship is an act of resistance; it helps us better show up for the world because it reminds us of who we are beneath this toxic programming. The fog has lifted, and all is clear to see it as it is. There is no unseeing the importance of fighting for racial justice, for the liberation of marginalized communities, and for the right to live in joy collectively.

Everything is alive, and everything is part of a grand Ceremony called life. There is ritual in everything we do and in everything we are, from the mundane to the magical. *Life is a Ceremony, and you are the ritual.*

# Self-Worship Prompts

These exercises can be done once a day or once in the morning and again in the evening. Try not to rush through them, and give each one your undivided attention: practice self-honesty and self-compassion. Give yourself space in between each one. Journaling is like having a conversation with yourself, tuning in and revealing truth.

Taking breaks from healing is essential. Remember to implement joy and fun into your life as you journey through this book. There will be things that come up, like aha moments, hidden memories, pain, fears, downloads from Divinity, and so much more. Take your time, best friend, you got this! Take a deep breath in, and exhale a huge *aaaoouuuuu!!!*

1. We all have hidden parts to ourselves that we don't share, often because we are trying to fit in, or we feel embarrassed or shameful, or we fear parts of ourselves. Others do not necessarily need to see these parts you hide, but it is important not to ignore or hide them from yourself. Let them be seen by you.

   PROMPT: What is a part of you that you keep hidden and why? No one is going to read this, so be honest; allow yourself to be vulnerable.

........................................................................................

........................................................................................

........................................................................................

........................................................................................

........................................................................................

2. When it comes to compassion, we often have a lot to give, but we miss the mark when it comes to ourselves. It is helpful to reflect on how much compassion you give and how much you can give to yourself.

   PROMPT: How do you show compassion to others, like your friends, family, and loved ones? How can you extend that same compassion to yourself?

........................................................
........................................................
........................................................
........................................................
........................................................

3. When we are in a bad place with ourselves or we are not happy with our lives, we often push that energy onto others and sadly sometimes mistreat them because of it. When we don't love or respect ourselves, it is harder to love and respect others.

> PROMPT: How can you better support and appreciate your loved ones? Have you done any harm you need to address or take responsibility for?

........................................................
........................................................
........................................................
........................................................
........................................................

4. Your inner child needs your love and care, and the best way to do that is by loving and caring for yourself now. There is a whole healing practice for the inner child, and I suggest giving it a go. One of the most powerful ways to connect to your inner child is by directly communicating with her.

> PROMPT: If given a chance to go back in time, what would you say to your:
> five-year-old self?
> ten-year-old self?
> fifteen-year-old self?
> twenty-five-year-old self?

Take your time with each of these questions and think of where you were at those times, what you were feeling and going through, what you needed to hear from your parents, what was said to you that molded you today, and what you wish you could have said to your inner child.

......................................................................................
......................................................................................
......................................................................................
......................................................................................
......................................................................................

**5.** Many of us play small when we should be playing big, taking up space, and showing up for ourselves—taking life by the wings and flying free.

> PROMPT: What area of your life do you feel you are playing small in? Why? What are you afraid of? What is the worst that could happen? What is the best that could happen? And now ask yourself, why are you running away from your ultimate potential and power?

......................................................................................
......................................................................................
......................................................................................
......................................................................................
......................................................................................

**6.** Self-honesty is a superpower to hone. It can be hard to admit to things that you do or don't do that cause harm or keep you from growth. However, once we become comfortable calling ourselves out on our own bullshit, mountains start to move.

> PROMPT: Are there any behaviors you currently have that restrict or block you from becoming your ideal self or manifesting your dreams? What are they? And what plan of action can you take?

......................................................................................
......................................................................................
......................................................................................
......................................................................................
......................................................................................

7. Most people don't feel seen by their partners, family, friends, or society. In-stead, they feel unappreciated and overlooked. When we start to discover our-selves, we no longer need to be seen as much by others. Though the people we love and care about should totally see us, maybe you need to start building a better support system if they don't. The more we discover the Divine Self within, the more others see us.

> **PROMPT:** Write down all the things you do for which you feel unappreciated and unseen. And then ask yourself: Why am I doing these things? For whom? Is this something I can stop doing? Is it important to me? And then read each one out loud say, "I am seen; I appreciate me."

88

......................................................................................................................
......................................................................................................................
......................................................................................................................
......................................................................................................................
......................................................................................................................

8. Celebrating ourselves is often overlooked. Whether our actions are big or small, we should celebrate all that we do, especially on days that are hardest. You can change your mindset from "I didn't do shit today and I'm feeling bad about it" to "I did what I could today and that's okay, I did my best." You don't always have to be "productive" to have a successful day.

> **PROMPT:** Make a list of everything you did today, from brushing your teeth to drinking a glass of water.

......................................................................................................................
......................................................................................................................
......................................................................................................................
......................................................................................................................

**PART**
**3**

# Self-Discovery

THEY SAY LOVING YOURSELF is the gateway to happiness, but what if we've gotten happiness all wrong? What if we've been pursuing the version of happiness sold to us by the systems that simultaneously oppress us? What if there is a crack in the mirror that has always made us believe the reflection is broken? In the pursuit of "loving ourselves," we have instead become obsessed with our own self-hatred. We don't see our flawless perfection; we see the things they tell us we need to fix. What if when we try to love ourselves, we just end up hating ourselves more? What if in the endless game of self-help and personal development, we only end up hurting ourselves and others?

These aren't over-the-top questions; these are common questions that get overlooked in most modern-day spirituality practices. And this becomes even more true when people come from a background of abuse, mental illness, or ethnic or economic struggle. How does their perceived brokenness get used against them? We are all different, and we all come from different cultures and lifestyles, so the practice of self-love might not be as hard for some as it is for others. In real life, I have yet to hear someone say that loving themselves is easy, but online, the spiritual community paints this flawless, almost enchanting picture of what loving yourself looks and feels like. Meanwhile, some of us are like, "I washed my hair today; that's as much self-love as I got."

That is why self-love cannot be done in healthy practice until we know how to truly worship ourselves and discover who we are. It's a journey, but the more we practice self-love, self-patience, and self-forgiveness, the more we are able to liberate the Divine Self within.

## 9

**DEVOTIONAL**

# The Journey
# of Self-Discovery

elf-discovery is a lifelong journey. It is the process of unveiling who you are without the layers of exposed falsehoods. From who you are to what you stand for, self-discovery encompasses the many truths that make *you*. By discovering who you really are and who you aren't, you will be able to liberate the Divine Self and create a life that you love, designed by you, for you.

In a world where we constantly compare ourselves to others and buy into what's trending or popular, we fill our lives with things that aren't what we genuinely like or want—creating a character that hides our true self.

The misconception around self-discovery practices is that they promise a destination, one purpose to uncover, one "you" to reveal. Bestie, if you can do one thing in this lifetime, make it about letting go of the false notion that we came here with one purpose and that we are on a journey to find it. Your purpose is to live your best life, and on that journey of life, you will discover who you are, and as you discover who you are, you will realize there are many seasons in your one life.

There are many codes embedded into our Souls. And those codes aren't secret or only revealed to a select few. You are already chosen, bestie. Stop seeking what you already hold within. Stop chasing, and allow what's meant to come, to come #divinetiming. You will wake when you are meant to, and there is no timeline or deadline. It will happen when it's supposed to.

As I learned, in order to discover the Divine Self, we have to surrender to the Magic of Divinity, learning to trust in her timing, lessons, and delivery. We are finally able to release ourselves from expectations, especially those from the spiritual communities who attempt to paint a picture of what our healing and spiritual growth journeys should feel and look like. Beware of those who try to teach "stages and phases" of the spiritual journey because they are not your truth. These are just beliefs made up to make sense of one's spiritual journey and, hermana, there is no sense to make of it. It is mysterious, unique, and still works perfectly for the individual on the journey. Your Divine Self knows what she is doing. Not everything needs to have an explanation because Spirit and Magic live outside of the confines humans continually try to place them in. These very beliefs are the blocks keeping you from abundantly manifesting and from deeply remembering, discovering, and connecting to your Divine Self. It is what keeps you from seeing yourself in truth and power and from truly seeing others.

*I see you because I can see myself.*

Self-discovery is a loaded phrase, and when I used to read it, I would feel both intrigued and apprehensive. In many ways, it served as a reminder of how much I really didn't know myself. Instead of being enlightened by the questions that were supposed to shine light on who I was, I would become anxious that I was never going to know. I ended up finding this to be true for many of the people I worked with, and I learned that their books, workbooks, and anything pertaining to self-discovery were often left undone. I also found that many people, including myself, just did not care to dig out the Divine Self. Why? Well, we are constantly dealing with so much in real life that an act like finding yourself seemed nearly impossible. It was more work than we had the time or mental capacity to attempt.

In addition, self-discovery can be triggering. Again, what I share with you does not mean it is true for all—we all come from different backgrounds, with different hurdles to overcome, but I can share my experiences in the hopes that you realize that this shit is not easy. Also (bad news, bestie), there is no one solution for all things. There are no quick fixes here. Instead, this work offers a powerful healing that can better your life and self in ways that support you while helping you to navigate through life's messy and often ugly parts. It brings you inward, where you are better able to see the beauty that life does offer and the unconditional love that comes from being in tune with Divinity—*your* Divinity.

This is why self-worship is essential in navigating through discovering who you are. Yes, we know who we are at a certain level, but who are we when we strip away all the programming? What happens when we slow down from hustle culture, when we heal, forgive, and find compassion, patience, and self-acceptance for ourselves?

*What self-worship does is build a mindful, caring, and loving relationship with ourselves as we are now so that when we move to discovering who we are deeply, we are armed with practices like self-care, love, and community to create a support system during our journey.*

While on the journey to self-discovery, we often find that we simply don't want to face certain aspects or parts of ourselves. This work can seem intrusive to the inner child, and so you may find it difficult to even ask yourself the simplest questions, like "Who are your role models?" or "What do you see yourself doing ten years from now?" I specifically choose these two because they were ones that sent me into a depressed state whenever I asked them.

You see, growing up where I did, where most humans around me were not good people (and struggling with things that no child should ever have to struggle with), I did not have role models. And in my present world, it felt like all the people I would consider role models were perfect, and in comparison, I felt unperfect. It was hard for me to accept that I didn't have just one person I could call a role model. It wasn't until I learned that *perfection* is a shit word, offered as a false standard by society, packaged and commodified to sell products, that I was able to answer the question. I began to realize that everyone I came into contact with who had good intentions toward me was a role model. They each taught me something through different acts of love and care, showing me how we can be and interact from a place of the heart. They showed me how every act of love is led by Spirit. And so my final answer is that Spirit is my role model, as are all the people who are led by her.

Where do you see yourself ten years from now? Ugh, seriously? I don't know what tomorrow will bring, and now we have to think about a decade from now? At the rate we're going, we might not even have a planet by then. Think about the entitlement that comes from projecting into a future that might look categorically different for each of us, based on the circumstances of our lives and Earth. I've always hated this question. I remember being in fifth grade and being asked it. All the children were beaming with excitement to answer, meanwhile I hid behind my big, puffy curls, praying I wouldn't be picked to respond. I was picked. #fml

I stood at front of the class, and immediately kids started to giggle, whispering "la bruja" (the witch) and pointing at my dirty shoes with holes in them. "Where did you get those?" they asked with disgusted faces. "The garbage bin. Dirty bruja, hahahahahaha . . ."

The sad part is, back then, teachers in neighborhoods like mine where primarily white, and most did not care if you were being bullied. I knew I was on my own.

I told myself, Deep breath in and exhale, Juliet. Okay, so where did I see myself in ten years?

I looked up at the class and yelled, "*Super* far away from you comemierdas!" (*Comemierdas* translates to "shit-eaters." It's a term mostly used by Cubans to call people "dumbasses" or "fools," but I meant it literally.) LOL—ay, little Juliet, how you inspire me today.

In order to heal through the trauma I experienced, including mistreatment by shit-eaters who didn't have compassion for a girl who was less privileged, I had to work through a lot of self-forgiveness in my adult life. Self-forgiveness opens up room for the parts of yourself that you have hidden for fear of being authentic, for fear of being vulnerable, for fear of being who you really are and connecting into the hard things you have experienced. I hid many parts of myself because those parts where abused, laughed at, bullied, and looked at as "other." We all have things we need to work through when it comes to self-forgiveness, but when you do the work, self-discovery becomes less triggering and more of something to look forward to.

*Self-discovery is a journey in which we continue to connect to ourselves, over and over again.*

I am not the same person I was ten years ago, and ten years ago, I wasn't the same person I was ten years before that, and ten years from now, I won't be the person I am now. The important thing to remember is that no one season is better than another. Each season awakens a different purpose within you.

In December of 2020, I died and came back a completely different person. And one of the only things that got me through the months that followed my death and rebirth was acknowledging that I didn't lose myself; I had just put that other self to rest and awakened a different part of me for this new season of my life and new purpose.

Self-discovery can unveil so many different things: what brings you joy, your values, your dreams, the things holding you back, your strengths and weaknesses, what you still carry from childhood. Meeting our Divine Selves for the first time can be scary; I mean, shit, Divinity is terrifying. However, you will also discover how fucking amazing you are—and how truly miraculous the Divine is when you let go of everything you think you know. I invite you to take this self-discovery journey with the intention that you find clarity and curiosity, mystery and wisdom, light and darkness, inspiration and growth.

To connect back to that Divine Self, we must begin to redefine how we see ourselves, how we love ourselves, the self-patience we deserve, and the self-forgiveness we require. As we uncover these concepts, we find how much of our thinking is rooted in old systems—family, cultural, political, economic—and we begin to realize that we cannot discover the Divine Self until we are willing to liberate ourselves from hate and shame and blame. When we finally begin to listen to the Divinity within, we find healing and the clarity we have always been seeking, the ability to hear the quiet but profound voice inside—the one that says, "I love you, bestie. Come right this way."

*There is only one you, and you are the only one that can unveil your truth.*

## Emotional Freedom Technique

Self-discovery isn't easy work; it can dislodge a lot of old emotions, toxins, and stress. It's looking into the parts of ourselves we've abandoned, the parts of ourselves we've refused to love, the parts of ourselves we've been impatient with, the parts of ourselves that we've failed to forgive. As you move through this work, I suggest you find ways to support yourself and the truths that may come back. Remember, your Divine Self loves all of you. There is nothing about you that is ugly or broken. You are beautiful, bestie.

To support your growth, I suggest trying Emotional Freedom Technique, or EFT, an important treatment I've learned that can help you balance your body's energy. Did you know that tapping on various acupuncture points can help you overcome anxiety, blocks, and worries in a short time? For me, it took a week or so to start feeling and seeing the changes and differences. I was so intrigued by this that I got my certification in EFT and have now been practicing with EFT for over a year.

I want to share EFT with you because it will come in handy for this work and the rest of your life. I ask that you please keep an open mind, bestie.

### So, What Is EFT?

EFT is a form of psychological acupressure used to treat a wide range of emotional and physical problems. This treatment sprang from the idea that all negative emotions are caused by a disruption in the body's energy system. It's a tapping sequence that helps release these energetic blockages. You will be using your fingers to tap on your body where your energy meridians are located. As you will find, it is a powerful tool not only for healing but also for manifesting and living a Divined life.

Recent research has shown that EFT significantly increases positive emotions, such as hope and enjoyment, and decreases negative emotional states. EFT is powerful for treating stress and anxiety because it specifically targets your amygdala and hippocampus. These are the parts of your brain that help you decide whether or not something is a threat.

I found that it has helped me so much with my stress and anxiety that I barely experience those emotions anymore. I have even used it to help calm my son's body in times of overwhelming emotions. And at the end of the day, I use it on myself to help my body relax. Combined with the rest of the work I have been doing in my practice, it has complimented my healing journey, and I know it will work for you too, best friend.

## How Does It Work?

First, you need to try to become present by taking two to three deep breaths. Focus on the emotion or issue you want to address. Then start the tapping sequence shared below while saying something along the lines of, "Even though I'm feeling [anxious] about [my book not being good enough], I completely accept myself anyway."

There are different ways to make your statements, instilling positive emotions with affirmations and positive phrases. See the QR code at the beginning and end of this book to access videos and other supplemental content for this section. I created a few EFT videos for different topics, but my favorite is the "Spiritual Baddie EFT" video. It's made especially for you, BFF.

You can do EFT whenever and wherever you like. I've done it while waiting in line to practice self-patience (more on that soon), and I love to do it in the mornings to shake up my energy and fill myself with positivity.

## Step One: The Setup

Locate the "Sore Spots" on your chest. They are below your collarbones, about three inches down and three inches over from the notch in your neck. To get your body's energy to focus on healing itself, rub your Sore Spots for two to three minutes. While you are rubbing, repeat this affirmation:

> "Even though I have this _____, I completely accept myself. I am doing the best I can."

Make sure to fill in the blank space with the emotion or problem you want to address. Infusing what you say with an intention or honest emotion is essential in helping you believe in your statements. Repeat the affirmation two to three times, being mindful of going slow and taking a pause between rounds.

Here are some examples of positive statements:

> "I was having trouble accepting myself, but I now know my Divine Self."
> "Even though I was feeling lost, my Divine Self knows where I am going."
> "I was feeling sad, but now I am feeling a new source of power."
> "I had a shitty morning, but the rest of my day is going to be amazing."

## Step Two: The Sequence

This is where the tapping comes in. Using your middle and index fingers, you will tap each of the following points seven to ten times, and you can use either hand or both hands at the same time. We will be moving downward from your crown, to make the sequence easier to remember. Each time you move to a new point, say a reminder phrase (for every 7–10 taps).

○ **Crown:** located on the top of your head in the center
○ **Eyebrow:** located just above the nose where the eyebrow starts, slightly to the side
○ **Corner of the Eye:** located on the bone alongside the corner of the eye
○ **Under the Eye:** located an inch under the pupil
○ **Below the Nose:** located in the area between your nose and upper lip
○ **Under the Mouth:** located below your bottom lip and above your chin
○ **Collarbone:** located where your collarbone and your first rib meet
○ **Under the Arm:** located about four inches below the armpit
○ **Under the Nipple:** located about one inch below the nipple
○ **Fingers:** located on the outside tip of each finger where the nail and the finger pad meet
○ **Karate Chop:** located on the fleshy, outside part of the hand between the top of the wrist and the bottom of the pinkie finger

Head to the QR code to find supplementary content on how to properly do EFT. Again, as you move through the contents of this this book and your life, make time to practice EFT, creating a safe and supportive space for your work and for your Divine Self.

# Discovering Self-Love

Quick story: A friend just called me on the phone while I was writing this, and she mentioned having a ton of things to do, but at that moment, all she felt like doing was taking a break for ice cream and Netflix. I was like, *yes*, that is self-love. Listening to yourself and knowing when to take a break and enjoy the moment *is* being productive. We need rest, pockets of joy, and moments of calm to connect with the Divine Self, the space from which true and productive creativity is born. #divinetiming isn't about luck; it's about matching the speed and flow of the Divinity within us. My friend's call reminded me why I am writing this book. It's to give you permission to redefine everything in your world—from happiness to productivity to self-discovery to self-love.

There can be many reasons for having a hard time with self-love and self-care. For so many of us, we've been sold a picture of self-love that looks one part rich white lady at the salon and two parts everything we need to do to fix ourselves. The idea is that we can only love ourselves through action, but what if the fastest way to self-love is through rest?

Before we go about redefining self-love, let's talk about love (period). I personally didn't really know what love felt like or what it was until the day I had my first son. It was an explosion of raw, instinctual, unconditional love I hadn't ever experienced. I was in my early twenties, and I still remember looking at his tiny face and thinking, So this is what love is. I started to cry and laugh hysterically. It was just so new to me, but it was also so very familiar in the most curious and mysterious way. I could not believe that I'd had so much love in me all that time, just waiting for an outlet. And this is not to say that my parents didn't love me, but the love they showed me came in the form of keeping us alive and making sure our bellies were full; tough love was the theme of my upbringing. I don't blame my mother for not having the time and energy to show me love in a more gentle and intimate form, but I also never knew how powerful and transformative love could be.

For so many of us, our understanding of love is limited by the definitions offered to us in childhood. We don't even need systemic forms of oppression to have been given fucked-up versions of love. But they don't help either. We believe that love is always conditional. It's based on what we do, how well we behave, how little we complain; it's centered on how we look or what we do or who we know; it's dependent on how much we give, how much we take, how much we are willing to sacrifice who we really are to fit someone else's conception of us.

When I held my son that first day, I just wanted to love him for all he was and was going to be. I didn't want to give him anything but the pure and raw magic of a mother's protection, nourishment, and nurturing. It took me many more years to wonder what it might look like if I offered myself that same protection, that same nourishment, that same nurturing.

But guess what? You also have love in you, even if you have never known it. Love is a part of who you are, and it is the most powerful presence interwoven into the very creation of you. We may not love ourselves because we haven't received the right form of love from others, but self-love is the devotional you deserve, bestie! And just like anything else, it takes practice.

Many of us have long believed that love can only come from outside of us. I remember the days when I would look for love without even knowing it, searching for it with every person who showed me the littlest bit of attention. Ugh, can we go back in time, please? Needless to say, those dates never turned out well. It is easy for people to manipulate you when you lack love for yourself, and sadly I did not know this when I was younger. This translated into my relationships as well; I was never truly happy and always felt like I was missing something. I thought love came from other people and that those people were responsible for my happiness, joy, and filling up my heart. #iblamedisney

And I do. Because this false happiness has always been a charade. You don't need no charming prince to come save you on his mighty white horse. You are your own savior and hero. You are your heart's truest love.

When we fall in love with ourselves, there is nothing and no one that can break that bond. What I began to realize is that self-love is about being the only one responsible for our happiness, the only one responsible for filling our hearts. The rest of the love that comes our way is a bonus.

As I've said, I grew up in a world where self-love, self-worship, and self-care were considered selfish, if not downright evil. The fucked-up part was that those messages didn't even come directly from my communities or my culture; they came from a capitalist society that showed only some people (white, wealthy, privileged) indulging in the acts of self-love and care and leaving my people to believe that it was not meant for them. Honestly, they weren't even easily accessible to BBIPOC communities as they were often priced at ranges that were and still are hard for people to afford.

And what was worse was that these ideologies were only further supported by colonial religions, telling us that self-worship was the devil's work. But this very sentiment is what separates most of us from Divinity in the first place—keeping us from finding true happiness within. We were supposed to work and have children and pay our bills and not fight back—or else, hija, what might become of you? #STFU

I don't blame my people; they were brainwashed into this mindset because here is what becomes of us: we heal, we rise up, we make demands, and we don't accept their oppression anymore. Don't let these people fool you, BFF! Love is the fabric of your *soul*. You are worthy of love, you are capable of loving, and you deserve to love yourself radically.

I spent decades not being able to accept myself. I had a love-hate relationship with my body and with who I was. I never understood where this was coming from, and it did quite a number on my mental health. But there was no therapy my parents could send me off to. I didn't have that privilege. "Aww, you feel bad?

Walk it off." That was my form of therapy—dealing with my ghosts and monsters on my own. In the end, they were often the only ones there for me.

This love-hate relationship still exists today, and I am not going to pretend that I have it all together and or that I am now this perfect spiritual being. Fuck no. It defies the purpose of this work, of this way of practice that I've been hollering about from the depths of my soul. But because of this practice, I know how to be gentle with myself, and I know that undoing and unlearning is a process that may never end. The journey is my focus and the source of my happiness.

You do not have to accept yourself 100 percent; this relationship is like any other. It needs time to blossom and gain confidence. Stay faithful to your truth and your emotions. This is the way to an honest relationship with yourself and a re-discovery of the Divine Self within.

Love is not chained to conditions; it is all-encompassing. And it is yours to give and receive.

Obstacles are to be expected on your journey, but they do not have to contribute to self-sabotage. So far, we have covered powerful lessons to help prevent you from giving up or not following through. But there are a few more challenges I want to talk about in this section that are probably the most prominent in your life. We want to work on setting healthy goals with purposeful intentions that inspire you, rather than goals that reach toward commodified happiness or "perfection."

*Perfection* is an evil word, if you ask me, and it's an evil that has been programmed so deeply into my subconscious that forty years later, it is still one of the most brutal monsters I face. Perfectionism is dehumanizing and locks you in a state of a never-ending war against yourself—it also capitalizes on our need to want to look and seem "perfect," selling us everything from beauty products to weight loss programs.

And that's not to shame anyone. Look, we all need a little "zhuzh" from time to time. You get to choose your own happiness, but you also need to make sure it is your choice and not influenced by something or someone outside of you.

To feel truly liberated, we must learn to let go of perfectionism, which, if you think about it, keeps you from truly being yourself.

I am imperfect and still worthy of love from myself. I am raw and bruised and yet I am still absolutely flawless. Cheers to those of you who carry ghosts and monsters within you and still try to walk in the path of Spirit; you are inspiring. It may not seem that way, but, best friend, if you are going to believe anything I say, consider this: The stars and mountains move for you, and if they seem to be blocking your way, it is because you have yet to acknowledge your own power. Instead of carrying their weight, move them out of your damn way.

Listen, self-love has so many layers to it. You don't have to be loving up on yourself on the daily to create a life where you are worthy of every good thing you desire. You are doing the best you can right now, BFF. But one of the most important things we can do is not compare ourselves to anyone else, ever. And the most powerful thing you can do for your own self-love and spiritual growth is to celebrate other people's wins, successes, accomplishments, and manifestations. You will not get anywhere hating on others, and, I promise, you don't want that kind of energy in your Spirit. If we can't find a way to open our hearts and let go of hate, judgment, and jealousy of others, it will be that much harder to be grateful for what we do have and to believe that what we can do is enough. When I see those people online living it up, I think, "Good for her! You get yours, girl!"

*Self-love is a unique journey for each of us;*
*if it looked and felt the same for us all, then there wouldn't be*
*any truth in the love we give ourselves.*

We've been divided and conquered for so long that we can't even see the canyons between us. The greatest act of revolution we can achieve is to come together. It's to love ourselves so deeply that we look at everyone with the same love we might offer our children. Because self-love is only one path to discovering the Divine Self. We also must begin to connect with the people who will support us.

## Support System

Whether you like it or not, your outside and online environments are just as important as your inner one. I know you are probably used to spiritual teachers being nice and gentle with you, but I'm not your spiritual teacher; I'm your BFF right now, and I need to be straight with you. Food is not the only thing that you ingest for nourishment; people, things, and places also nourish you, and just like certain foods, they can also be toxic. Your outside environment may not be something you have control over in terms of location, housing, and living arrangements, but you can control who your friends are, who you choose to be in relationships with, and what you digest online.

I met this wonderful lady at one of my favorite plant shops one day who recognized me from social media. She had just purchased my book *Plant Witchery*, and she told me that she was at the plant shop because after reading the first few parts of my book, she was inspired to get out of the house. It was too hot to go for a walk at the park, so she thought outside of the box and came to this gorgeous two-acre plant market that's indoors and a lot cooler than outside. Apparently, I never got the notice that shopping for plants is a form of connection to the Earth and also self-love and self-care. (And I won't even share how many times a month I go because you will say I have an addiction. #ido LOL) Why didn't I think of that!?

This woman instantly made me feel like I was winning at life. Then she told me that she'd taken a quick look at her Instagram account just a few minutes before spotting me and had seen a picture of someone she follows that made her upset because it was about fat shaming. Apparently, this person fat shames a lot, and she was triggered. She started to cry and then set down the plant that she had been holding in her hands.

That's when I said, "Oh hell no!" startling the poor woman. No one should ever be made so sad that they put down a plant. I gave her a huge Caribbean hug, and then I grabbed her hand and led her around the market until I found the perfect spot—ah! I sat my butt on the ground by the cacti and said, "Sit down, bestie, we have some talking to do."

I asked her, "Why are you following this woman?"

She explained that she wanted to get motivated to change her bad habits.

I responded, "And her triggering you is good for you how?"

Sometimes, all it takes is an outside perspective to see how we our poisoning our insides. The woman told me that she hoped this influencer would make her want to change.

This is what I told her, and it's what I am going to tell you right now if you need to hear it: "Bestie, listen. She is no good for you if she makes you feel bad about yourself. First off, following anyone who shames anyone is not good for anyone. Being bigger or curvier isn't a fucking thing to be ashamed of, period. You are gorgeous! No one decides what body shape is ideal and beautiful. Goddess made us all beautifully unique, and you do not need to change a damn thing to feel good about yourself."

Ugh, I probably need to repeat that back to myself because I understood what that woman was going through. Generally, I do okay feeling good in my own skin, but then I am triggered, and it makes me fall off. I see something online, and it feels like I am taking ten steps back every time I try to move forward.

I know it's hard, but one of the most significant changes you can make that will impact and support your journey is unfollowing people who make you feel bad. When was the last time you went through your following list? Let's do it together.

I want you to unfollow anyone who makes you feel less than or triggered or anyone who drains you of your energy. Be mindful that people aren't necessarily toxic or not good for you because they have a different lifestyle, but if those same people are actively making you feel like shit, not supporting or respecting your goals and boundaries, then unfollow them. #byebitch

Your support system can be anyone or anything you want, but keep in mind that this support system should actually be supportive. Find people on social media who genuinely care and show real support, who don't cause harm. Evaluate who you hang out with, who you follow, and who you give your energy to. Find people in your life that you think would be good at being there for you and have a conversation with them; open up and ask if they would be willing to be part of your support team. (Can't find anyone? Or want to have me as part of your support team? Text me! Join my Spiritual Baddie BFF text community for free at 201-903-9150, or see your welcome package via the QR code, which has a direct link if the phone number doesn't work for you.) As you consider your support team, ask yourself:

○ Does this person support me?
○ Does this person respect me?
○ How does this person make me feel?
○ Is this person adding to my journey or holding me back?

Apply these questions to places, social media, and so on. There are so many *amazing* people online who are absolute lights in this world. I believe in being mindful of what I digest: people, music, TV, social media, and places. I try my best to keep them all vibing as high as possible, so they support and nourish my journey. Don't have good friends? Get out into the real world and make some. Go to places you love and do the things you enjoy. The people you vibe with will be the people who align with the things you believe in, love, or are interested in. And it's those same people who will help you on your journey to self-discovery.

In a way, it goes back to that cracked mirror. We see our Divine Selves in the reflections of others. And when they offer us a broken version of ourselves, we don't get to connect into our Divine powers; instead, we just see brokenness. But when we look in the mirror of someone who loves and believes in us unconditionally, we begin to feel that same love that I felt holding my baby boy. We feel protected, we feel nourished, we feel nurtured.

We see all that we are and all we are capable of being.

*Creating a life you love, and one that supports your growth, requires that you reevaluate what doesn't and does nourish your mind, body, and Spirit.*

_____

# A Daily Self-Love Shower Meditation

This meditation is to be done in the shower (audio version available via the QR code):

Close your eyes and take three deep breaths.
Start to count backward from ten to one in your mind.
Focus on your breath.
Breathe in and breathe out.
Listen to the soft songs of your breath, in your nose and out your nose.
Feel your chest rise and fall as you inhale and exhale.
Relax and now feel the waters rain over you,
releasing tension and washing away negativity from your head,
your eyes,
your nose,
your mouth,
your shoulders,
your arms,
your chest,
your tummy,
your back,
your hips,
your legs,
your hands, and your feet.
Feel yourself settle deeper into relaxation, and allow the sacred waters to embrace you.

And then envision:
Imagine standing under a waterfall. There's someone on the other side of the waterfall walking through waters toward you.
You realize that this someone is you, your Divine Self. Take a moment to visualize what she is wearing, how she smells, and what her energy feels like.

She asks you, "Are you ready to love me?"

When ready, put your hands up to meet hers and say, "I am ready."

You both start to speak in synchronicity as she holds space for you and supports you in embracing yourself.

Repeat:

> I love you.
> I love you.
> I love you.

> I love your heart.
> I love your bravery.
> I love your resilience.
> I love your strength.

> You are extraordinary.
> You are magical.
> You are sacred.
> You are a miracle.

> I love your body.
> I love your laugh.
> I love your ambition.
> But most of all . . .

Take a deep breath and now hold each other.

> I love your uniqueness.
> I love your flaws.
> I love your mistakes.
> And all your dark parts.

Take a step back and hold hands, take a deep breath, and just gaze into your eyes. Feel your Divine Self filling you with authentic deep love from your feet all the way up to your crown.

Listen as she says to you:

> I love everything about you.
> And even though you are always evolving, growing, changing, and shedding what no longer serves you, you are getting to know me a little bit more every day.
> I love you.
> Just the way you are.

Close this meditation when you are ready. Say thank you, and slowly open your eyes.

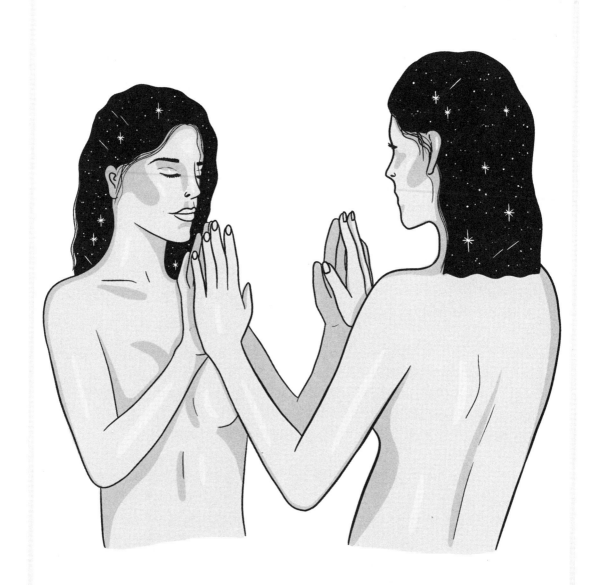

# Discovering Self-Patience

Like many of us, I had impatient parents, teachers, and caretakers when I was a child. As a result, I grew up feeling rushed in almost everything I did or had to do, carrying this awful fear of not getting it done right or on time. Because I was rushed back then, I now get anxious when I am rushed today. I've worked through this for a few years, and I've come incredibly far! I set boundaries and learned to be patient with myself, and I've disconnected the voices of the past from my mind. But let's be honest, this shit is hard work.

What I quickly discovered is that it's easier to show patience to others and that I seem to run thin on it when it comes to myself. Some of you may not even know that you don't have patience for yourself because it has been a part of how you think and function for most of your life. We beat ourselves up and critique our every move, expecting ourselves to do things perfectly or achieve crazy goals or accomplishments in short amounts of time. One of the main reasons I left social media and my work behind for this long was to step out of the hustle culture and into the slow ritual of living.

I've met many people who I've worked with who feel like they are not doing enough or not achieving things fast enough. And in most cases, this feeling can be traced back to their upbringings. However, not all lack of self-patience comes from there. In fact, our whole system has been built to promote and maintain hustle culture.

I am not against working hard, but I believe in working smarter, not harder. I also believe that you gain so much wisdom from and love for what you do when you let things take time, when you give yourself space to rest and recover. Look, I get it, honie, we got bills to pay—and the gas company doesn't care about your self-care—but how much more do we really make from hustling? And how much do we lose? There is a difference between having to work hard to survive and forcing yourself to join the popular hustle culture to make shit happen right now.

And that's what I've #canceled officially from my life. Because before you know it, this journey will be over. And you will have given little presence to your life because you have been stuck in the grind. Even for those of you who do have to hustle to survive, it is still important to take time for yourself, to give your mind and body downtime. No matter how busy you are, you can take time to slow the fuck down. Just remember that self-care and love does not look the same for everyone, so do what works for you.

And the crazy part is, the more you trust Divine Timing, the more the universe responds. You see, Divinity works on an infinite timeline; she doesn't have a Passion Planner or a Google Calendar. She is busy wandering the forest, pressing the leaves to her face. When we slow down for her, we can finally hear her message, and we can finally understand what she wants for us and how we can achieve it. I manifest like a boss; always have. It's like my superpower, and I can tell you that hustling has nothing to do with it.

*Manifesting has everything to do with your relationship with self and Divinity, not with the amount of work you do or how "productive" you are.*

Learning to be patient with yourself takes practice; it isn't an overnight thing. So basically, you need the patience to practice self-patience. No worries, bestie, just take it one day at a time. You got this! Take a deep breath and tell yourself that it's going to be okay.

Self-patience is freeing, and it is the most beautiful form of gentleness and grace you can give yourself. Practicing self-patience helps you accept yourself and give yourself love and care. When we are impatient with ourselves, we create stressful and anxiety-driven thoughts and harmful life patterns. When we practice self-patience, we feel much more at peace internally and externally.

And perhaps when you are in a space of self-patience, you can actually sit down under the tree with your Divine Self. You can talk for hours, listening to her gentle, loving, and supportive guidance. You can begin to discover her and understand how long she has been waiting for you to see that you were your Divine Self this whole time; you just needed to slow down enough to greet her.

## Practice the Art of Waiting

In order to practice self-patience, we must learn to wait. You can consider this your anti-Karen exercise—no asking for the manager and demanding your pancakes now. Don't worry, Divinity is whipping up a major stack, but first, you must learn to wait for sweetness. Practicing the art of waiting helps build your muscle memory for self-patience. But also, it's a wonderful way to develop mindfulness, slowing down our desire to consume.

Here are a few ways I implement waiting:

○ Not reaching for my phone first thing in the morning. I fight the urge and wait about an hour or two. I leave my phone alone until I have finished my morning rituals. Building that space in the morning has helped me to change my trigger to reach for devices. You will be surprised at how much more time you have when you stop always grabbing for your phone—in the morning and throughout the day.

○ Staying away from impulse buying. This was super hard, bestie! In a world where with one click you can quickly buy just about anything, it is hard to be patient and wait a day before purchasing. I now wait for a least a day before going back to buy what I want, and most often, I save myself a lot of money because I have different feels about the item the next day and I don't end up buying it.

○ Changing my attitude about lines. Ugh, who doesn't dislike long lines? I used to be that person who would stand in line and just look miserable, glaring over at the register and giving a stank look at those taking their sweet-ass time. I decided that if I have to wait in line, I have to make it work for me. So I developed patience by telling myself to breathe, knowing that we all get to the register soon enough. I ask myself, "What's the rush? Everyone is trying to do the same thing I am, and no one needs my crap energy while already having to wait in line." I'll close my eyes and repeat mantras and affirmations, I'll pull out a book, or I'll listen to music or a podcast—anything to keep me calm and help the time go by.

There are many ways to implement waiting into your daily life that will super-power your self-patience. And guess what, BFF? The more we become mindful in our waiting practice, the more we discover what we want and how we want to spend our days. Instead of getting mad in line, we can check in with that Divine Self, have a chat, cool our heels, and know that we don't get to enjoy the journey when we're rushing through it. When we pay attention to the things we want to rush through, we get incredible insight into who we are and where we're going. Asking ourselves "What's the rush?" can slow us down enough to let go of the rush.

## Be Grateful

I know, I know. How many times have you been told to be grateful? It's like being told to wake up at 5:00 a.m. or drink more water. And though all these things are wonderful suggestions, they can feel meaningless unless we understand their purpose. You see, gratitude is actually one of the most powerful ways to unlock self-patience. Practiced regularly, gratitude will not only ground you and bring you more joy and happiness, but it will also help you to slow the F down.

I love to journal daily on what I am grateful for. It helps me center myself and appreciate even the tiniest things in my life. Sometimes it's challenging to feel grateful or find something to be thankful for when times are hard, but there is always something, and keeping a daily gratitude journal will help you become better at being mindful of all the beautiful details in your life.

Below, I've created a list of daily gratitude journaling prompts that you can choose from to use for your own gratitude journal, but don't feel pressured to use them. I personally love to follow prompts—sometimes I use the same ones over and over again—but you can also journal on what you are grateful for without any prompts. There are no rules about how you should keep your daily gratitude journal!

Start simply: begin with one or two questions from the list below and keep journaling for the next thirty days without skipping a day. I prefer to write in my gratitude journal in the evenings as a nightly ritual. If for any reason I miss a day, I do the prompts for the day I missed the following morning. You can choose whatever time of day works best for you. Here are twenty-five daily gratitude journaling prompts:

○ What are you grateful for today?

○ What is the biggest gift in your life right now?

○ What magic did you find or experience today?

○ What small thing happened today that you're grateful for?

○ List at least five things you like about yourself.

○ Describe your favorite moment of the day.

○ What is something a friend or family member did today that made you grateful for them?

○ Name a struggle you currently have. What about that struggle makes you grateful?

○ Write about a recent obstacle you faced and how you overcame it.

○ What is one aspect of your health that you're grateful for?

- Write about a pet and what makes him/her special.
- What about the current season are you grateful for?
- What are you thankful for in nature?
- What positive changes in your personality have happened in the last year?
- What about your body are you grateful for?
- Describe a piece of positive news you recently heard.
- Describe your happiest childhood memory.
- What is one of your favorite songs from your childhood?
- Describe a family tradition that you are grateful for.
- Describe your favorite location in your house and why you like it.
- Describe your favorite smell.
- What is a great book you've recently read?
- Write about a random act of kindness from another person that you've experienced.
- What is something you're grateful to have learned this week?
- Write about something you are grateful for in your work or personal life.

*Gratitude expresses or shows appreciation for what you have right now, for the people and friends in your life, and for the things that show you kindness, love, and magic. Gratitude is being mindful of and thankful for all the good things that are available to you at this moment.*

If you practice patience every day by being mindful, slowing down, being grateful, and delaying instant gratification, you'll become better at self-patience. With this patience, you will start to be kinder and more compassionate with yourself and others, which will help you in your spiritual development and growth.

# Discovering Self-Forgiveness

To forgive yourself is another powerful and beautiful form of self-discovery. Forgiveness is an essential step to letting go of the past that may be haunting your present—and that is likely hiding you from the Divine Self within. It is important to note that self-forgiveness is not condoning, excusing, or minimizing; instead, it is about taking responsibility and accountability so you learn from past experiences to move forward. When we allow ourselves to be free from the things we haven't forgiven, we are able to see ourselves in our most flawless forms, the people we can be when liberated from our pasts and our mistakes.

*When was the last time you took a deep breath? Take a moment to do so now, and on the exhale, release a big sigh: aaahhhhhh.*

But on the other side of that, if we avoid self-forgiveness, we can do enormous harm to our mental health and nervous systems. Self-blame and shame have been connected to anxiety, depression, and a weakened immune system. I can personally attest to this. I had no idea that I needed to forgive myself, and, honestly, I didn't know what that meant or what it would even look like. But as I mentioned earlier in this book, I used to have a ton of anxiety and fear, my physical and energetic bodies were taking a beating, and it wasn't until I started to do this devotional that I saw the correlation between the work I was doing and the healing that was starting to manifest.

So what exactly is self-forgiveness? Having a clear definition of forgiveness and what it means to you is an essential first step. It can mean different things to different people, but one thing it isn't is creating a confessional where all your "sins" are forgiven. This isn't about sin. This is about acknowledging our truths, faults, and poor choices, just as we should acknowledge our positives. There is no shame in being human and making mistakes, but we also shouldn't hide poor decisions that may have caused harm. They will show up in your life in other forms, through emotions, or relationships, or your health.

Forgiving yourself is about more than just letting go, putting the past behind you, and moving forward. It is also about accepting yourself and showing yourself compassion. What you need to forgive may be something minor, or it may be significant; again, we are all different, and what you may need to forgive will be different from what someone else does.

For me, one of the things I needed to forgive was the way I punished myself when I did not accomplish something. For instance, whenever I wanted to drop weight, I used to diet, not realizing that each time I started, it was another road to self-punishment. You see, I would start and stay on track for a week or two, and then something would happen, and I would spiral out of control with food. I would feel like shit and hate myself for being lazy, inconsistent, and not dropping weight. This pattern repeated every time I started and "failed"—a vicious cycle. I did not physically harm myself, but emotionally I was abusing myself the whole time.

Doing this devotional helped me to see things from a different perspective and opened a shit ton of worm cans—or is it cans of worms? (Insert thinking emoji here.) The healing journey isn't pretty. It is ugly, harsh, scary, and downright agonizing at times. It isn't easy to go down the path of self-forgiveness, but, best friend, it is worth it. Imagine the caterpillar and the journey it has to go through to become the butterfly. Get those wings, bestie; they will look super fab on you!

# Mid-Book Break from Healing

Get yourself some crayons or paints and a canvas or paper you can draw on (feel free to use the space provided on the next page). Draw what you would like your wings to look like. Be as detailed as possible—include colors, shapes, textures, and patterns. They can look however you like (you may already have envisioned them). Don't worry about being perfect or not being a good artist #imnot LOL; give it a try and have fun with it! I would *love* to see your wings, so please tag me on social media @iamjulietdiaz and use the hashtag #thealtarwithin.

Draw Your Wings

# Learning to Forgive Yourself

All right, let's get down to the good stuff. Here is the simple four-step process to forgiving yourself:

## *Acknowledge What You Did*

This is the hardest part of self-forgiveness: facing the truth. You can't learn, heal, or grow from mistakes or unhealthy choices unless you acknowledge them. Take responsibility, but also don't place blame or judge. We want to avoid being unkind to ourselves. Think about what happened and why. What was your role in this? Asking yourself these questions and reflecting on what happened can help better prepare you to avoid doing it again. Gaining wisdom out of shitty experiences is how you turn a negative into a tool for positivity.

## *Apologize*

When you do something that may have hurt someone else, you apologize. The same applies to yourself. Be genuine about the apology, and feel into the words you tell yourself. I found that writing an apology letter is what worked best for me. An apology letter to yourself can be as simple or as extensive as you like, as long as you're genuine with your apology. Here is an example:

Dear Juliet,

I've never written a letter to you before, and now that I think about it, I wish I had. Getting to know you and communicating with you more has been the best decision I've ever made. It hasn't been easy, and it's even been painful at certain points, but you are totally worth it!

I've done things in my life consciously and unconsciously that have brought you harm, like the times I was unkind and harsh with my thoughts and words toward you. You have been through it all with me

125

and have never let me down, and I am so sorry for being so fucked-up when things didn't go as planned. I want you to know that you are pretty badass and extraordinary. When you fall, you get back up, always finding a way to rise even when the fall breaks you. I am sorry for the way I treated you when you needed me the most—when you needed love, when you needed care, and, most importantly, when you needed me to be there for you.

The things I said to you came from brokenness, yet you still showed up for me to put the pieces back together. I promise that I will be kinder, more compassionate, more patient, and more understanding with you. You are my ride-or-die, after all, and I will do everything in my power to protect and love you for the rest of our lives.

Thank you for being resilient and persistent even through the times I hurt you the most. I am deeply sorry and apologize from the depths of my heart.

Love,

Me

### Focus on What You Learned

Focusing on what you learned instead of what went wrong will prepare you for going forward and will help keep you from repeating the same mistake. Knowing what you did and the consequences that came from it gives you wisdom. For me, from the cycle of dieting and being hard on myself, I learned that I was looking for a quick fix, and instead of bettering myself, I was doing more harm than good. I learned to appreciate taking my time to achieve my goals and wants, developing self-patience, self-compassion, and a self-love relationship with myself.

### Make Meaningful Changes

To avoid repeating the same experience, take what you have learned and apply it to how you can make changes in yourself and your life. I took the time to educate myself on nutrition and how certain foods affect or impact my mind and body. I also worked on loving myself more and appreciating my body, so I didn't feel the urge or need to jump into a diet whenever I gained a little weight. I unlearned harmful behaviors around food and rid my mind of the programming of what a "perfect body" should look like. Instead, I started to become an activist for beauty and celebrating our bodies for being different and unique.

We all make mistakes, and we all make bad choices; that doesn't make us weak, and it doesn't make us any less capable of loving ourselves. Life is literally a school with lessons meant for us to learn. Self-forgiveness is ultimately how we come to discover that Divine Self. We are free from the blame and shame. We can throw off the belief systems that drove our self-hatred and self-fear. So many of us have lived in the dark silence of our bad decisions. We're too afraid to tell anyone what we've done, and instead, we disconnect from who we truly are. But I promise you, bestie, no matter what mistakes you've made, you can connect back into the Divinity within; you can emancipate yourself from shame or embarrassment.

And you can look back at those mistakes and choices and use them to fuel your activism and change-making in this world. If you had problems with drinking or drugs, you can use your story to inspire others. If you struggled with depression or diet culture, you can share your pain so that others know they're not alone. If you fucked up because we live in a fucked-up system that limits our choices and freedoms, you can use your accountability to fight that system.

This isn't about blame. And this shouldn't ever be about shame. This is about responsibility and the deep and unconditional love we can find for ourselves when we finally learn how to self-forgive. From the small stuff to the big things, no one can tell you what they are but you. It takes self-honesty to look at your past and study yourself. To liberate the Divine Self, you must discover who you are and where you need healing, love, and care.

# Setting Self-Discovery Goals

S elf-discovery is a practice within itself, and now that you have gone through different parts of the whole to successfully create solid foundations, we can start to set some goals. Don't worry, we're not going to create some impossible to-do list with crazy-ass deadlines. No, these will be simple yet effective goals you can set on a daily basis to help you in your growth. I created a simple thirty-day self-discovery challenge for you to use, but before we get to that, let's talk about why and how setting self-loving goals is essential to your spiritual development and well-being.

Look, self-discovery can feel uncomfortable and awkward at first. Have you ever started dating someone who you were super into? You're just getting to know each other, your palms are sweating, you don't know what to say, and you are too scared to look them in the eyes? Yeah, well, self-discovery can look like that too. And that's okay. We are not trying to fake the process. We want to be our full selves as we begin to discover our Divine Selves. Remember to practice self-love, self-patience, and self-accountability. Let's go, bestie!

*Self-discovery is a bridge to where you want to arrive.*

I've tried to be mindful of the things that are often missing on the journey to "awakening." Too often, we're told that the path to wholeness, healing, and

Divinity is a simple nonstop journey. But it's not. It involves planes and trains and hiking and resting and dancing around. Your commitment to self-discovery is a crucial part of having a fulfilling, magical, and impactful journey to mastering the Divine Self and living your best life for the rest of your sacred days on this Earth.

Self-discovery is possibly the most important presence in setting goals with intention. How can we know what we're capable of achieving, and at what pace we are supposed to move, unless we're in deep understanding of our Divine Self? It's why we live in so much disappointment. We tell ourselves we need to get married or find a partner, have children or reach some career goal, buy a house or a car or whatever, all by a certain age. But if we really tune in to the Divine Self, if we are willing to listen to her whispers, we will find that life happens in the most Divine time, not in our time.

The key to setting self-discovery goals is to make sure they align with your beliefs, values, and who you are. They have to have intentions backing them up that are meaningful to you. Setting goals and planning is where many people fail to realize that goals without intentions will backfire—and this often causes people to give up on them. You must do things because *you* want to, because they are in alignment with your Divine Self, not because someone or some part of modern life tells you to.

This is why I made this practice a devotional to Self rather than a set of instructions that tell you what you need to do. Reading this book is lovely, but unless you are putting the devotionals into action, they are just words on a page. I am your guide, but you are the keeper of your Divine Self and the one holding the power.

Here are some tips for setting goals:

- ○ Whatever your goal is, it is crucial to your success that you have a clear idea of why it is important to you. Writing down goals is the easy part, but it's the intention and the why that matter the most. Your goals should be things that motivate and inspire you to stay consistent.
- ○ Establish some form of tracking your progress. We often get so hung up on seeing significant changes overnight that we miss the magic already

happening to get us there. Find a way to measure your progress, not in a quantitative way, but in a qualitative way. Are you feeling freer? Are your shoulders lighter? Do you have more hope and excitement and joy? Appreciate every small step toward your bigger goal.

○ Make sure you are realistic about the goal's timeline. Back to my experience with dieting (sigh): I used to be so unrealistic with my weight-loss goals, and part of the problem with being consistent was the ridiculous timelines I would set for myself. I am being completely raw here because I want to be real on the shit we put ourselves through: I would set a goal of losing five pounds a week! Like WTF, Juliet, I was literally setting myself up for failure before I even started. At the time, I honestly thought that I could accomplish that, mainly because I believed the nonsense most diets preach. But I held myself accountable and was honest with myself in the part I had in attempting such a goal. I now know that I was secretly and subconsciously sabotaging myself. This is why this work is so life changing: because it gets into every nook and cranny of your being. You are on #divinetime. No matter what you want to achieve, through self-discovery, you will become more aligned with the magic of your process.

*When one practices self-discovery,*

*one becomes a mirror.*

A loving reminder: Remember, you are perfect just the way you are. The intention behind setting self-discovery goals should not be to fix or change yourself but to better understand your spiritual, mental, emotional, and physical well-being. They should help you reconnect to the Divine and reclaim your truth, identity, power, and sacredness, not from others but for yourself.

# Thirty-Day Self-Discovery Challenge

For this thirty-day self-discovery challenge, you need to write each of the thirty prompts below on individual pieces of paper and then fold them up. Place them all in a bowl or jar and mix, mix, mix. In the morning or evening, stand in front of your self-discovery bowl or jar, close your eyes, and pick out a piece of paper. No cheating, bestie. The prompt on the paper is your challenge for the day. *Have fun!* I'm so excited for you! Please make sure to tag me on social media (@iamjulietdiaz) with your challenges and #thealtarwithin. I cannot wait to see each one of you self-discovering your Divine Self in all her amazing Glory (insert heart emoji here).

1. Watch your favorite movie. Remember why you love it.
2. Buy or pick flowers for yourself today. Why do these flowers speak to you?
3. Repeat this affirmation ten times: "I accept myself exactly as I am now."
4. Compliment yourself in the mirror. What compliment would your Divine Self offer?
5. Massage your hands with lotion or oil for ten minutes. Imagine they are the hands of your Divine Self. What do they feel like?
6. Go for a walk in nature. What does your Divine Self notice? Where does she want you to focus your attention?
7. Put your feet up and close your eyes for fifteen minutes. Be still, and ask your Divine Self what she wants to say.
8. Have a picnic lunch. What does your Divine Self want to eat?
9. Make a new friend in the real world today. Find a friend that reflects the Divinity within.
10. Do not use social media today.
11. Take five pictures of things you find beautiful or magical today. Ask your Divine Self to guide you.
12. Put your favorite tunes on, and dance with your Divine Self.

13. Create a bucket list today. Ask your Divine Self what she sees for you.

14. Sit in silence for ten minutes near candlelight with your Divine Self. Be silent together.

15. Spend fifteen minutes massaging your feet. Imagine they are the hands of your Divine Self. What do they feel like?

16. Lotion your entire body. If you're comfortable, do it in front of a mirror. What would your Divine Self say about you? How would she appreciate your body?

17. Enjoy a bubble bath. You can even imagine your Divine Self pleasuring you. How would she touch you?

18. Buy a plant. Ask your Divine Self which plant she would choose.

19. Repeat this affirmation ten times: "I accept love from myself."

20. Do yoga for at least twenty minutes (YouTube has amazing yoga teachers). Imagine your Divine Self helping to move and guide your body.

21. Get a manicure and/or a pedicure (yes, men as well!).

22. Compliment a stranger. What would your Divine Self notice about someone else?

23. Stay away from negative people today.

24. Live it up today. Do what brings you joy. Ask your Divine Self what she would like to do.

25. Create a playlist of songs you and your Divine Self like. What soothes her?

26. Write your Divine Self a love letter.

27. Go on a date with your Divine Self. Where would she want to go?

28. Look for or ask your followers on social media for accounts they love that inspire and empower them. Earlier in the book you unfollowed people but now it's time to add magic back into your feeds.

29. Dress up today. How would your Divine Self want to be seen— without judgment, fear, or worry?

30. Repeat this affirmation ten times: "I am discovering my Divine Self."

# Self-Discovery
# Is the Road to Liberation

More than ever, I believe that the most significant and most essential journey we take is discovering who we really are. For most of our lives, we are bombarded by both the inner critic, who is constantly giving us all the wrong ideas about ourselves, and by the outside world, telling us who we are, where we should be, and what we should wear, eat, and listen to. When did the world become a colossal puppet show? Oh, I know, when the colonizers came through and started implementing ideas, laws, and systems that would take us away from who we are—stripping away our identities, which then stripped us from our power and liberation. And the game hasn't changed; just some of its players have. And some of them might even look and act and talk like you; they make you believe that they know what you need and that they have just the right thing to fix it. Fuck that, bestie, you deserve to be you, all of you, however that feels good. You don't need other people defining your liberation.

When you find yourself, you learn what works and what doesn't vibe with your Spirit. This is crucial in moving forward into a life that supports you fully, one that offers more joy, love, and good vibes without the fluff and bypassing.

We get to ask the most important question of all. Who am I *really*?

Self-discovery is an act of self-love and self-care that leads us to the root of everything we do and are and believe. It reveals our truest essence, the Divine Self. Through it, we ask ourselves, What do we value? What are our priorities? Are those priorities serving us or hurting us? It is a process that involves breaking us down to the bare minimum, shedding layers that do not serve us and don't reflect who we really are. We start to recognize the self and mindfully build ourselves up, which, instead of provoking anxiety, creates an excitement for the possibilities of tuning in to your truth.

Without self-discovery, we can't recognize our power. Research has shown that it isn't just the things that happened to us that define who we become; it's how much we've made sense of those things.

Through self-discovery we are able to make sense of our past, cutting the noise of our trauma to start hearing our Divine selves. This is an important act of self-discovery because through Divinity, we start to realize what we are aligned with and what we aren't. We become liberated from who we think we are to create a life we love, a life that is led by Spirit. You can then identify the practices and rituals that suit you best, uniquely created by you, for you.

In this space, we find true happiness and deep healing, not the kinds sold to fix us, but the happiness and healing we all have inside, which, when we access them, finally free us.

## Burning Ceremony

The Burning Ceremony is one of the most freeing experiences I've ever had. It was something I "accidentally" created that ended up changing my life. I was having trouble discovering who I was because I was too attached to who I thought I was. Self-discovery isn't about what we think about ourselves; it is about what we know. If we do this work from our brains and not our Spirits, it will become a constant battle to move forward while holding on to the old self, old habits, and old beliefs. The Divine Self isn't interested in our shit. She knows how much we have to do and what we think and what we're afraid of.

A couple of months ago, I was sitting on my bed and started to look around. In the corner of my room was my workspace with my computer, which I hadn't touched in months, piles of books, papers, folders, vision boards, planners, lists, and unread mail. I thought to myself, WTF have I been doing these last few years? I practically lived in that space and was always working. Mind you, I work for myself—I have my own business and brand. But that didn't stop me from overworking myself daily #fuhustleculture. I did take time off to go out into nature here and there, but I always came back to work even harder, undoing the rest and recovery. It was a harmful cycle. Who was I doing it all for? Why wasn't it ever enough? When was I planning to celebrate my wins and honor true rest? Why didn't I believe I deserved it?

*I was having trouble becoming who I wanted to be*
*because I was too attached to who I was.*
*So I laid her to rest. Then I was reborn.*

I felt this rage building inside me, and then everything went black. I lost my shit. (After that awakening, I was unhinged for a few months, and this was just one of those days.) I started to take everything off the table and threw it on the floor. I looked down and realized it was my "burning pile." I was constantly creating all these plans, just adding more to the already-busy days I used to have. My calendars, planners, and lists all went into the pile.

I then headed to my bookcase and took out every single book that I had in there that I knew I would never read and had no interest in anymore, which emptied half my shelves. (Don't worry, I donated them. What do take me for, some kind of monster?)

Next was my closet. I had more clothes in my closet labeled "for when I get skinny" than I could actually wear in that moment. So out they went, into the donation pile. I grabbed anything and everything that didn't feel authentic to who I am, asking, Why do I have this? Why did I get this? Most of my responses made me realize that I never genuinely wanted these things but that they fit with the character I had created, one I wasn't even connected to anymore.

I found my vision journal and started to read through it, and all I kept seeing was wishful thinking and no real depth. Were these things what I truly wanted? Or were they what society says we should have, attain, and dream? I swooshed them into the garbage bin, which by now was overflowing and spilling over into that burning pile.

Then I found my medical records: blood work and tests. They were a reminder of how unhealthy I was. Tossed those into the burning pile. The pile was now up to my waist, and I was still going, sweating, panting, crying, and screaming. There was a top shelf that I could never reach without a ladder, but there was no ladder in sight, so for a moment, I thought, "Leave it be," but then I remembered what that pile was. It was piles of cut-out magazine pictures, clippings of things I wanted to try and places I wanted to see, like an undone heap of life goals and bucket lists just sitting there for when I had more time to organize and fulfill them. They had been sitting there for four years, and I had yet to find the time. It wasn't a vision board; it was a nightmare. But I was going to fix that right up, so I climbed up my bookcase and balanced my footing, right leg on the shelf and left foot extending to the cabinet about three feet away. I tiptoed and stretched all the way up until, finally, I reached the papers, and suddenly everything came toppling down, including myself, and I landed in the burning pile. #ofcourseidid

I laid there in silence for a moment to take in what had just happened, and then it hit me; I landed just where I needed to. This extraordinary laughter rushed out of my soul. I was now crying and laughing at the same time, and it was fucking blissful. #surrendered

I took this pile outside and sat with some paper in hand. I decided that I wanted to burn all the things that my inner critic would say to me along with that pile, including a list of old beliefs and old habits that were causing me to think about my life but fail to live it.

Dreams and visions and plans and goals are all wonderful. They can be expressions of who we are, but they aren't our true selves. The Divine Self isn't a pile of clippings at the top of your closet. She isn't bloodwork or magical planners. What I realized was that none of that stuff was me; I was so much more powerful than the ghosts that I was housing within myself.

Adding myself to that pile was the best mistake I ever made. It held me accountable for the mess I had created, and as I sealed my letters in an envelope and placed them on the burning pile, I knew I was now ready. *Flick*, I opened the lighter, and I set it all to flames. I then grabbed a blunt, lit it up with the flames of the burning pile, and smoked while I stood there until it all became ash. #litasfuck

Here's how to do a Burning Ceremony without losing your shit (or burning down your house):

- ○ List all the things your inner critic says, all the things that were ever told about you that aren't true and that bring you pain.
- ○ List all the things that were ever done to you and that keep you chained to their ghosts.
- ○ Make a list of habits you want to get rid of or change.
- ○ Write a letter to those people who hurt you and tell them how much they caused you pain. Let it all out.
- ○ Gather things that can't be donated that you want to let go of because they belong to someone you are not.
- ○ Find a safe place where you can't cause harm with a fire. Place all your things, including the letters, in a pile there, and light it up!
- ○ Allow yourself to go through the emotions and let them all out. Scream, cry, or laugh if you want to. Just allow yourself to be.

Note: Please be mindful of Mama Earth and don't burn anything that's plastic or contains chemicals. Wear a mask, and give yourself enough space between the fire and where you will stand. Have a fire extinguisher handy just in case it is needed. Also be mindful of laws in your town. Under the age of eighteen? Please have parent supervision.

# Sacred Truths

You did that, BFF! I am so proud of you for taking the time to sit with yourself and practice these devotionals. Whether your truths are positive or hard to face, it is important to be able to trust yourself in discovering them and exploring who you are. My hope is that you take away from this the practice of self-communication and that you implement it into your daily life. Conversations with yourself are vital for moving forward in life, and they allow you to connect with your Divine Self.

Wow! What a journey so far. Let's take a moment to take three deep breaths in and out. Give yourself a great big hug, bestie. Take a day off from healing and do what brings you joy; then come back to begin the final devotional: self-activism.

*The most beautiful thing you can wear*
*is your authentic self.*

# Self-Discovery Prompts

**1.** Every person you have met has created a different version of you in their mind. It is not your responsibility to correct those versions of yourself because they don't belong to you. What you can correct is the version of yourself that you created in your mind to hide your true self.

> **PROMPT:** If you wrote an autobiography, what story would you tell? Who are you in this story? What are your characteristics, personality traits, likes, and dislikes? How do you feel? What do you look like? What do you like to wear, eat, and listen to? Be as specific as possible.

..................................................................................................

..................................................................................................

..................................................................................................

..................................................................................................

..................................................................................................

**2.** Learning from our past is essential in arming ourselves with Divine wisdom moving forward. Dwelling in the past isn't good for you or your well-being, but putting its lessons to good use for the present and future will help you let go of the negativity of the past.

> **PROMPT:** What do you regret the most? What would you do differently if given another chance? Imagine you could travel back in time to speak to yourself after this experience. What would you tell yourself? (Best friend chiming in here: Maybe practice self-forgiveness? xoxo) And how can you use that lesson to shift how others experience their own pain?

..................................................................................................

..................................................................................................

..................................................................................................

..................................................................................................

..................................................................................................

3. Sometimes it's hard to see the strength it took to get ourselves through hard times. We focus on the difficulty of it all and forget to celebrate ourselves in overcoming.

> PROMPT: Think of a time when you were able to overcome a difficult situation. Describe the situation. What strengths did you use to get through it? What did you learn about life and yourself after the experience?

..............................................................................................
..............................................................................................
..............................................................................................
..............................................................................................
..............................................................................................

4. Beliefs about ourselves are often rooted in our life experiences and by what others have said to us—embedding them with our identities. They can be empowering (e.g., "I am smart") or disempowering (e.g., "I am not good enough").

> PROMPT: What experiences in your life have created your beliefs about yourself? How have your family, culture, and economic and political systems amplified those messages? Think about a belief you've been taught in your life. Is this belief accurate? What would it feel like to release these false beliefs about yourself?

**Examples of negative and positive experiences and beliefs:**

**Experience:** My mom was hyper-focused on weight.

**Belief:** If I am skinny, I am beautiful.

**Experience:** Effort was often praised in my family.

**Belief:** I am capable if I put my mind to it.

..............................................................................................
..............................................................................................
..............................................................................................

........................................................................................

........................................................................................

**5.** Comparing yourself to others is harmful to your well-being and can spiral out of control, making you feel less than, jealous, and resentful. Instead, we can find those who inspire us and empower us to be better and do better for ourselves, and we can admire them.

> **PROMPT:** Think of a person you admire and explain why. Why does this person resonate with you? What values and attributes do they have that you can apply to your life?

145

........................................................................................

........................................................................................

........................................................................................

........................................................................................

........................................................................................

**6.** Books and movies can have a significant impact on us, especially when we are young. I remember learning about healthy family relationships, lessons, and values from TV shows like *Family Matters*, *Full House*, *Bewitched*, and *The Addams Family*, to name a few. When times were hard at home, books, TV shows, and movies gave me hope for what could one day be.

> **PROMPT:** Talk about a book, TV show, or movie that had a positive impact on your life. What did you learn? How did it change you?

........................................................................................

........................................................................................

........................................................................................

........................................................................................

........................................................................................

7. Willpower is something we can conjure up, but the energy backing our willpower withers away after a certain point, mainly because we don't have purposeful intentions supporting the actions we are trying to accomplish.

> PROMPT: What are some things you keep trying to accomplish but can't complete? Ask yourself why these things are important to you and why you want to accomplish them. Don't be vague. Truly find the roots of what drives you if you want to achieve them. And then ask yourself the hard questions: Why do I keep falling off? And what can I do to stay committed?

.................................................................................................................
.................................................................................................................
.................................................................................................................
.................................................................................................................
.................................................................................................................

8. When trying to discover our Divine Selves, we need to unlearn and liberate ourselves from the stories and narratives forced upon us. If we don't, it is hard to create a vision of who we truly are. By being mindful of the things that do not belong to you, you can eliminate the blocks keeping you from connecting to the Divine.

PROMPT:
1. Describe yourself using the first ten words that come to mind.
2. Pinpoint where each of those words is rooted from.
3. List ten words that you'd like to use to describe yourself.
4. List a few ways to transform those words into reality.

.................................................................................................................
.................................................................................................................
.................................................................................................................
.................................................................................................................
.................................................................................................................

# Self-Activism

OMG, bestie! Look how far you've come! #spiritualbaddie

We are now coming full circle, as all good things do, because self-activism asks that we create a clear vision for our future selves and life while harnessing the will to realize that vision. It is just as I dreamed for you at the beginning—this is your great and important opportunity to step fully into your Divinity, your power, and to become fully present within yourself. We learn how to master ourselves when we get out of our own way, stripping away who we aren't and activating who we really are. And yes, it is a powerful form of activism to become who you are. It requires a committed devotion to self as you continue the journey to self-liberation, healing, growing, and living a life your ancestors would be proud of. By doing this work, you are also preparing yourself for the life you are calling in, for the manifestations, so that you are able to fully acknowledge and accept what you deserve to receive. It's a process of waking your becoming.

Self-activism is realizing the different parts of yourself that make you whole. Each one is sacred and important and plays an essential role. Bestie, here's the real truth: everything you seek lives within you. Despite your histories and traumas, you own your moment. No one else is responsible for you but you. Self-activism isn't about control or domination. It's about a deep understanding of the Divine, transcending the systemic oppressions while learning how to break through your own resistance to celebrate the sweetest, most knowing parts of your Spirit. Because the most powerful form of activism in the world is celebration.

# The Power of Self-Activism

S elf-activism is when you start to do things on your own terms for reasons you choose, rather than because of what others want you to do or be, especially the capitalist society in which most of us live. When we let go of mindless actions and reactions, digging deep into our intentions and meaning, we start to lead with Sprit. We become leaders.

But first, we have to do the hard work—stripping away the parts of ourselves that aren't in alignment with Divine Self, so that we recreate and rebuild more solid foundations, support, and practice from within and without. Through this practice, we have the incredible opportunity to embrace ourselves and discover who we really are, realizing the different parts that make us whole, honoring the sacred parts while transcending the parts that resist change. Ultimately, self-activism is about persisting toward change, plugging you fully into Divinity as you begin to know and trust your Divine Self.

Why is this so important? Well, if I haven't convinced you yet that being you—the true you—is life changing, then let's talk about the other side of activism: living your Divined life. So manifestation and magic are not only my jam; they are also everyone's birthright. I'm about to make a whole lot of people mad AF, especially some of the publishing giants and wellness spaces who make big bucks off of "teaching you" how to manifest the life you always wanted. It's a growing and thriving online business as well, with tons of people selling courses, programs, and services to help you manifest like a boss. Ugh, deep breath.

Ready, bestie? Okay, so what if I told you that the true magic of manifesting literally lives within you? The true you. The Divine Self. Meaning there is nothing more to do other than focus on your spiritual, emotional, physical, and mental well-being to help you tap into your manifesting power and make shit happen. I know it's not easy, as I've explained throughout the book, but that doesn't mean it has to be complicated. Because here's the real truth: there's no one way of manifesting, there is no blueprint, there are no laws or trickery, there is no having to high vibe all the time or matching your desired intentions to manifest what you want.

You don't need the expensive courses and programs, you don't need to learn the "law of attraction," you don't have to look in the mirror and chant phrases taught to you by some white lady in one of those fancy felt hats. All you need is you, activated by *your* truth. Look, we all know the feeling—that deep space where you can feel the Divinity within. Stop reading right now. Close your eyes. Listen to that silence within. It's in that space that you are able to manifest because your wants and needs are clear, you are communicating with the Divine, and so your Divine Self brings it forth.

There's no hocus-pocus and there are no scientific explanations that will help you create magic in your life better than being authentic to yourself. Real magic works from within, and everything else is a tool with which you can amplify the intentions you want to set. This is why candles can be powerful for some people. They are my best tool to work with because I have found that, for me, they work. The law of attraction may work for you, but it is not the reason why you are manifesting—it is only a tool. *You are the magic.*

And the magic happens when you enter into this space of self-celebration, the joy in being you, in knowing you, in vibing with your own energy. Are all those things they sell you about manifestation true? Well, that's up to you to decide. Has it been working for you? Like, really working? If it has, bonus! But watch how tapping into your Divine power explodes enchantment in ways you never would have imagined.

As you enter more deeply into that Divine space, the things you want to manifest will begin to change. You will start to ask yourself, Is having a fancy, expensive car really something I want? Is having an expensive-ass condo in NYC something I dream about? Or do I want these things because the manifesting communities tell me subconsciously that luxury items and expensive lifestyles are the manifestations of the truly worthy? Those things might be right for some and that's okay, but I'm concerned that luxury, rather than liberation, has become the gold standard of manifestation.

I'm not shaming those who want these things, but I am inviting you to think about what is really driving you. Where are your desires coming from and why? I believe I am able to manifest because the things I want to manifest are rooted in truth; they are born of my heart and Spirit. They are not driven by consumerism, media, or anyone else's vision of what a perfect life should look and feel like.

I've met amazing people who have incredible shops, businesses, and jobs, and yet they don't feel like they are up to par because they can't or haven't yet reached the expectations of what social media has painted as successful. And that breaks my heart because success is not someone else's manifestation; success is what *you* Divine. If you feel happy and have joy in what you do, then you are a success, bestie! At a large or small scale, it is your definition of success that matters. So let go and liberate yourself; you are already holding all the power. Reclaim it, take it back, call it in, and protect it. That magic is sacred, and it belongs to you, no one else.

## The Problem with Manifestation

Most manifestation courses, programs, and services charge big bucks, and they claim they manifest because they are raking in millions of dollars. That isn't manifesting; that is strategic marketing that capitalizes yet again on the hopes and dreams of hard-working, big-dreaming, spiritually-seeking people. Same shit, different packaging. Although some of these "teachers" are good-hearted and may mean well, they are still part of the capitalist systems that are more harmful than helpful. You do not need to pay someone hundreds or thousands of dollars to get inspirational advice or learn the same things that have been taught over and over again throughout the years. It's the same information, the same "laws," the same fluff and #inspo simply resold and backed up by their personal stories of struggle to wealth.

Not to say that these teachers didn't make it (in their own definition of what making it means) or that they didn't work hard or struggle themselves. However, painting a dream that people wish they had and then using that as fuel to fill your own pockets is questionable.

I've seen this toxic AF advice from mainly white privileged manifesting teachers who say that if you want to be rich, you have to act rich. #thefuck

So people buy into this belief and spend their money on cults (yes, I'm calling them cults) that keep you trapped in their high-vibing, all-is-rainbows-and-unicorns hype poison. I've met way too many people who have lost everything falling for these dangerous marketing ploys. The things is, I've fallen for them too.

One year, I felt like I wanted to tune up my own manifesting powers. Here's the funny part: I am a master manifester, but I bought this program (for way too much money, I'll add) that was supposed to teach me how to apply my manifestation powers to my money skills. I wanted to see if there was something more to it than what I was already doing because the program claimed new methods and techniques. Sounds good, right? I mean, just because I know how to make things real doesn't mean I always know how to manage money. I was a perfect pawn. I spent a lot of money to be taught the same manifestation lessons that have been around for years; they were just packaged differently. And I learned what I already knew: nobody but me can control my own financial decisions.

I'll say it again for you: nobody but you can control your own financial decisions.

See, for too long the manifestation communities have acted as though they are responsible for your manifestations. You sign up for their programs, something good happens in your life, you come back and share it with the community, and then the teacher takes credit for it, as though "their methods" made it happen. More people see this and then join in on the hype. In the end, you were the one responsible for the financial decisions that made your life better or easier or more interesting, but your participation in the program made that teacher richer. When things don't work out for people, the teacher tells them, "Look, don't despair. Manifesting takes time. You just need to fix your attitude and let go of limiting beliefs." And in the end, the student ends up paying, waiting, and digging bigger holes in her bank account.

The sad fact is that 80 percent of people who spend money on these programs end up spending more money than they can afford, getting them into a harmful cycle that only leads to some realizations and a whole lot of despair.

Listen, manifesting does take time, and some manifestations are quicker than others, but the essential thing to know is that manifesting has nothing to do with these teachers' methods and everything to do with tuning in to yourself, practicing self-worship and discovery, and aligning with your truth. That truth drives your manifesting magical powers. When your desires and dreams become filled with mindful, authentic intentions and clarity of self, you begin to take the steps to reach those desires and dreams.

Do I want to call this out? No, not really, but someone has to. And I am tired of seeing my people fall due to the systems of oppression that are hidden in almost every aspect of our lives.

But when we focus our energy on unchaining and liberating ourselves from oppression, the magic of self-activism starts to happen. Self-activism is the practice of self-worship and self-discovery implemented into your life. It is taking your power back and reclaiming what is yours while also dismantling your wants and needs from the capitalist, colonialist systems that drive so much of modern manifestation culture. When we learn to define our own goals and make our own paths toward those goals, we find the quality of life we actually want and need.

## Twenty-One-Day Practice of Self-Activism

I created a simple twenty-one-day practice of self-activism with the intention to help you practice what you've learned in this book and bring you closer to self, to Divinity, to *you*. It's a guide of sorts that can give you an idea of how you can create little challenges in your days to help you implement the practices and rituals that best support you. Have fun, don't take it too seriously, and, most importantly, find pockets of joy.

With all of the work, healing, rituals, and practices we covered in this book, you can feel confident in your journey; now you can begin to implement these things into your personal life and practice, manifesting like a boss, creating the life you desire, and navigating life while unveiling a little bit more of your authentic Divine Self each day. You can take breaks between days—make sure to listen to your mind, body, and Spirit when rest is needed. This practice touches on all areas of your life, amplifying clarity and vision.

Don't forget that #goodvibesonly #positivevibesonly is a delusion and a harmful way to try to live your life. Good vibes and positive vibes are the goal, yes, but not if we're spiritually bypassing our truths in an attempt to achieve them. When we avoid being harmful to others and ourselves, we are able to connect into our fullest growth, healing, and Divinity. You might recognize some of these practices from earlier in this book, but manifestation requires commitment and repetition. You are learning a new language, bestie, and it's the language of your Divine Self.

## Day 1: Funeral for the Old Self

A funeral for the self is not as grim as it sounds, nor is it a judgment of your old self. Its purpose is to put to rest a season of your life so that you may be prepared to celebrate the new one. Creating your space is the most important part. You want to create a space that is meaningful and purposeful. I am going to share how I created mine, and you can take from it what you like. You can put your own spin on it; there is no wrong or right way of doing it.

### WHAT TO DO

First, I set up my funeral space. I did mine by a river, but it can be done at home or wherever you like as long as it is a place that is distraction-free. I used cigar smoke and burned some sacred herbs from my ancestral practice and culture to cleanse the space (you can use whatever you feel connected to). You don't need to burn smoke to cleanse; you can also use sprays, essentials oils, bells, or whatever works for you. I set out a circle of white candles to sit in the center of. In the center, I sprinkled flower petals; I used white rose petals, lilies, chrysanthemums, and carnations, all of which are flowers often used in funerals, and all of which carry a beautifully loving and gentle vibration. I then lit the candles while setting the intention of protection and love.

Next, I wrote a letter to my old self. In this letter, I expressed my gratitude for having journeyed with her and learning the lessons that I did. I thanked her for being there with me through the good times and the hard times. I made sure to let her know that she will always be an important part of my life and that because of her, I could move forward to this new season of my life. You can write whatever you like, however you want. You can also address the parts of the old you that you will not be taking with you, like harmful habits, patterns, thoughts, and so on.

Once done, I sat with the letter for a few minutes to connect to my words and intentions. I then spoke these words out loud to Divinity (you can speak in your mind if you prefer and adjust this statement or create one of your own):

# The Power of Self-Activism

Dear Divine, I am ready to let go of my old self and move forward into the new season of my life, reborn and awakened to my truth. Thank you for that season of my life, the lessons I have learned, and the wisdom I have gained. My eyes are open and awoken to the possibilities I have the power to conjure.

Then I cut the letter into small pieces with a pair of scissors (symbolizing cutting the cords to the past and the list of all the things I wanted to let go of). I placed the paper in a burn-safe bowl and set it on fire. Once the fire settled, I blew out the candles one by one (if they blow out on their own, no worries). Finally, I made sure to wet the ashes and clean up my space.

# Self-Reflection Journaling

What did you learn or gain from this experience today?

...................................................................................................
...................................................................................................
...................................................................................................
...................................................................................................
...................................................................................................

158

Did you receive any downloads or experience any aha moments?

...................................................................................................
...................................................................................................
...................................................................................................
...................................................................................................
...................................................................................................

Write three things you are proud of yourself for today.

...................................................................................................
...................................................................................................
...................................................................................................
...................................................................................................
...................................................................................................

Write three things you are grateful for today.

...................................................................................................
...................................................................................................
...................................................................................................
...................................................................................................
...................................................................................................

## Day 2: The Self-Vision Board

A self-vision board is so much fun! You can create your vision on a board, paper, journal, Pinterest, or however you like. I'll share what I did below. The purpose of the self-vision board is to compile images, words, sayings, poems, cutouts, and whatever else you'd like to represent the vision you have for yourself. This does not mean the vision others have or expect from you; this is 100 percent your vision.

### WHAT TO DO

I chose a cork board I could pin things onto and could move around easily. (I especially like this because I can keep reusing the same board. You can decide what works best for you.) I then mindfully created a list of attributes, values, habits, likes, hobbies, aesthetics, and clothing I wanted my future self to have or enjoy. Then I looked for images, affirmations, poems, sayings, magazines cutouts, and printouts representing those things and pinned them onto my board. I also chose scents, textures, and symbols to add to the board to personalize it to my liking.

The self-vision board helps you set a clear vision of your intentions and what you desire. You are not working on your life here; that comes later. For now, focus on the future version of yourself.

# Self-Reflection Journaling

What did you learn or gain from this experience today?

.......................................................................................................................
.......................................................................................................................
.......................................................................................................................
.......................................................................................................................
.......................................................................................................................

Did you receive any downloads or experience any aha moments?

.......................................................................................................................
.......................................................................................................................
.......................................................................................................................
.......................................................................................................................
.......................................................................................................................

Write three things you are proud of yourself for today.

.......................................................................................................................
.......................................................................................................................
.......................................................................................................................
.......................................................................................................................
.......................................................................................................................

Write three things you are grateful for today.

.......................................................................................................................
.......................................................................................................................
.......................................................................................................................
.......................................................................................................................
.......................................................................................................................

## Day 3: One-Month Self-Care Plan

Planning for your self-care is sexy AF. But here's a little secret: if you don't make time for it, then you will not find time for it. Making self-care a priority can be challenging, but with mindful planning, you will be able to fulfill your self-loving plans. I personally plan out one to two months in advance, but it took me time to get to that point; I suggest taking it one month at a time at first.

WHAT TO DO

Get yourself a self-worship planner or calendar, or print out a free PDF (see the QR code for the "Self-Worship Planner" PDF).

Write out your responsibilities for each day, making sure to add any appointments you have coming up. Then, to each day, add something that you consider self-care, big or small.

When I have a busy day, I make sure to schedule something I can do quickly, like a ten- to twenty-minute meditation or five minutes of breathwork. I also add repeating daily rituals and practices. When I have more time in a day, I try to go big (and going big can mean different things to different people). I like to schedule spa days, spin classes, hikes, brunch with *good* friends, visits to the plant market, or facials. Having these activities planned out will help you follow through with them, but please note that if a particular day comes and you do not feel like going through with something, it's okay to rest instead.

# Self-Reflection Journaling

What did you learn or gain from this experience today?

.................................................................................................
.................................................................................................
.................................................................................................
.................................................................................................
.................................................................................................

Did you receive any downloads or experience any aha moments?

.................................................................................................
.................................................................................................
.................................................................................................
.................................................................................................
.................................................................................................

Write three things you are proud of yourself for today.

.................................................................................................
.................................................................................................
.................................................................................................
.................................................................................................
.................................................................................................

Write three things you are grateful for today.

.................................................................................................
.................................................................................................
.................................................................................................
.................................................................................................
.................................................................................................

## *Day 4: Honesty Mirror Exercise*

Be honest with yourself about the things that you are lacking, and then fill your heart with affirmations and words that you would like to hear yourself say more often. Self-honesty does not equal ungratefulness or negative vibes. It means you are one with yourself, and your aim is to grow, not to half-ass your spiritual growth.

### WHAT TO DO

Sit in front of a mirror, one where you can at least see your face.
Take a deep breath.
Close your eyes and take another deep breath.
Once you are ready, open your eyes and honestly answer the question below.
Allow yourself to speak out as you feel called to. Do not hold back. Be *honest*.

*What do you wish you would say more of to yourself?*
(Start with the statements that follow and then continue with your own.)

○ Know that you are good enough.
○ Know that you have gotten me through the most challenging times in my life, and for that, I am grateful to you.
○ Know that I am sorry for the horrible things I've said and thought about you; I will never hurt you again.
○ Know that I see you, I hear you, and I will never shut you up or hide you ever again.

# Self Reflection Journaling

What did you learn or gain from this experience today?

.................................................................................................................................
.................................................................................................................................
.................................................................................................................................
.................................................................................................................................
.................................................................................................................................

Did you receive any downloads or experience any aha moments?

.................................................................................................................................
.................................................................................................................................
.................................................................................................................................
.................................................................................................................................
.................................................................................................................................

Write three things you are proud of yourself for today.

.................................................................................................................................
.................................................................................................................................
.................................................................................................................................
.................................................................................................................................
.................................................................................................................................

Write three things you are grateful for today.

.................................................................................................................................
.................................................................................................................................
.................................................................................................................................
.................................................................................................................................
.................................................................................................................................

## Day 5: Become the Observer

Becoming the observer of your own self and life is powerful. It allows you to not be a reactive person but to instead mindfully address different situations from a place of Divine wisdom, self-compassion, self-honesty, and self-love.

### WHAT TO DO

Today you are here only to observe yourself. So take notice of when you are triggered—for example, anytime you start to feel sad, angry, fearful, jealous, lonely, and so on. Allow these emotions to happen, but then immediately take your focus back and make a note of what caused or triggered them. Do not skip this reflection about any of these emotions throughout the entire day.

Since you will be reflecting on these emotions right after you experience them, choose to journal at the end of the day. Then go over your notes and reflect on these emotions in a calm state. Say thank you to your emotions for showing up, and promise that you will no longer ignore them. Let them show up and acknowledge them.

This is the start of you working *with* and not against yourself.

# Self Reflection Journaling

What did you learn or gain from this experience today?

........................................................................................
........................................................................................
........................................................................................
........................................................................................
........................................................................................

Did you receive any downloads or experience any aha moments?

........................................................................................
........................................................................................
........................................................................................
........................................................................................
........................................................................................

Write three things you are proud of yourself for today.

........................................................................................
........................................................................................
........................................................................................
........................................................................................
........................................................................................

Write three things you are grateful for today.

........................................................................................
........................................................................................
........................................................................................
........................................................................................
........................................................................................

## Day 6: Becoming Your Own BFF

Imagine becoming your own best friend, your own go-to person when you need to be uplifted, the person with whom you share your day. You are your emergency contact. Your Divine Self is waiting for you to acknowledge and communicate with her. The more you learn to connect with self, the more you connect to Divinity (God)(Spirit). I talk to myself *all* the time. You will be surprised at how great you are at giving good advice and helping yourself through hardships.

### WHAT TO DO

Sit with yourself and have tea, coffee, or, my favorite, cannabis. (I sit and have a chat with myself almost daily.) Act as though you're having a girlfriend over and you are unloading all the things you want to share, release, and even gossip about. I don't particularly like to gossip, but the way I intend it in this context is to share what's been going on, including things at work or things someone did. If you find that you start to become negative about others or life in general, remember to reply as your Divine Self. This is a conversation, so it goes both ways. Spend some time getting to know yourself, have fun with it. This is a great way to tap into your own wisdom.

# Self-Reflection Journaling

What did you learn or gain from this experience today?

........................................................................................
........................................................................................
........................................................................................
........................................................................................
........................................................................................

Did you receive any downloads or experience any aha moments?

........................................................................................
........................................................................................
........................................................................................
........................................................................................
........................................................................................

Write three things you are proud of yourself for today.

........................................................................................
........................................................................................
........................................................................................
........................................................................................
........................................................................................

Write three things you are grateful for today.

........................................................................................
........................................................................................
........................................................................................
........................................................................................
........................................................................................

## Day 7: Freeing Dance

Today we *dance*! When was the last time you danced wild and free, like no one was watching, without any judgment from yourself or caring about whether you looked good or not? So much is pushed on us, from how we are supposed to act to how we are supposed to look, but *fuck that*! Free yourself from the chains that hold you down. Be you, unapologetically.

WHAT TO DO

Put on your favorite songs or playlist and pump up the volume. Yes, you can wear headphones if you prefer!

Dance for a minimum of three songs. Go for songs that you can lose yourself in and that get your body moving.

Dance alone, with the kids, with pets, or with whoever you like.

Do *not* judge yourself.

And most importantly, be wild, be free!

# Self-Reflection Journaling

What did you learn or gain from this experience today?

....................................................................................................................
....................................................................................................................
....................................................................................................................
....................................................................................................................
....................................................................................................................

Did you receive any downloads or experience any aha moments?

....................................................................................................................
....................................................................................................................
....................................................................................................................
....................................................................................................................
....................................................................................................................

Write three things you are proud of yourself for today.

....................................................................................................................
....................................................................................................................
....................................................................................................................
....................................................................................................................
....................................................................................................................

Write three things you are grateful for today.

....................................................................................................................
....................................................................................................................
....................................................................................................................
....................................................................................................................
....................................................................................................................

## Day 8: Self-Celebration Ceremony

A Self-Celebration Ceremony is something I do every six months, but you can do it as often as you like. Its purpose is to celebrate who you are and to honor yourself for your resilience, will, efforts, triumphs, and strength, even during the hardest of times. You deserve to be acknowledged, appreciated, celebrated, and worshipped by you.

### WHAT TO DO

Write a gratitude letter to yourself, highlighting what you're grateful for. (For example, you might include statements like: "I am grateful that I am able to feed my children and take care of my family.") Serve yourself your favorite food and drinks; buy yourself some balloons, flowers, or cake; try something new that you have been putting off; or keep it simple and chill by the candlelight, reading your favorite book or consulting your tarot or oracle cards while drinking your favorite wine, tea, or beverage. Whatever you do, make it special for you.

You can celebrate alone or with friends. In fact, you can make this a Celebrate *Us* Ceremony, where you celebrate everyone invited. Your guests can bring their favorite dishes to share, or you can all go to a restaurant that you love or have wanted to try. Have a toast to the importance of who you are. And don't forget to take pictures and post with the #thealtarwithin and tag me @iamjulietdiaz; I would love to repost and celebrate you, bestie!

# Self-Reflection Journaling

What did you learn or gain from this experience today?

......................................................................
......................................................................
......................................................................
......................................................................
......................................................................

Did you receive any downloads or experience any aha moments?

......................................................................
......................................................................
......................................................................
......................................................................
......................................................................

Write three things you are proud of yourself for today.

......................................................................
......................................................................
......................................................................
......................................................................
......................................................................

Write three things you are grateful for today.

......................................................................
......................................................................
......................................................................
......................................................................
......................................................................

## Day 9: Liberate-Spirit Ritual

Liberating your Divine Self will allow Spirit to lead you through life. It's like having your very own internal Spirit almanac without any interference. I found this ritual to be especially powerful in times of fear and uncertainty; it allowed me to break through resistance and to allow Spirit in. It can be done daily, which I recommend. Try to do it before meditation, before using divination tools, or when you need clarity ASAP. Where did I learn this ritual? I'm a seer, and in a vision, I saw myself doing this with my ancestors around a fire.

### WHAT TO DO

1. Get a candle (I prefer red, but you can use what you have available). Light the candle and place it somewhere near you but not too close, as you will be swaying your arms.
2. Sit on the ground, close your eyes, and envision yourself under a willow tree. She is shielding you, protecting you, and rooting you.
3. Think about the thing you need clarity on.
4. Start by taking a deep breath through the nose and holding it at the top of the breath for five, four, three, two, one, and then release it through the mouth. Repeat two more times.
5. Then start to take quick breaths in through the nose and out through the mouth in a rapid rhythmic pattern; repeat this eleven times. You may feel a little dizzy and you may receive a sudden burst of energy.
6. Bring your hands in front of yourself in a clapping position.
7. With your hands cupped, clap quickly fifty times.
8. Hold your hands slightly apart and allow the energy ball between them to vibrate for five, four, three, two, one.
9. Then scan yourself with this energy, starting from your head and working your way down. Repeat this three times.
10. Now that you have filled yourself with this energy, start moving and swaying your body, arms, and head wildly while letting out howling

screams or sounds (whatever needs to come out). Do this until you feel a release. Afterward, place your hands on your thighs to ground yourself. Start to breathe normally and be still. Keep your eyes closed and wait for Spirit to come through.

# Self-Reflection Journaling

What did you learn or gain from this experience today?

........................................................................................
........................................................................................
........................................................................................
........................................................................................
........................................................................................

Did you receive any downloads or experience any aha moments?

........................................................................................
........................................................................................
........................................................................................
........................................................................................
........................................................................................

Write three things you are proud of yourself for today.

........................................................................................
........................................................................................
........................................................................................
........................................................................................
........................................................................................

Write three things you are grateful for today.

........................................................................................
........................................................................................
........................................................................................
........................................................................................
........................................................................................

## *Day 10: Manifesting Flower Ritual*

This manifesting flower ritual holds a lot of intention and mindfulness. It is an Earth and Spirit ritual that communicates your desires to Divinity and Divine Self. This ritual can be done once a month, on any day or at any time, but I prefer to do it on a full moon under the moonlight. If there is not a full moon today, do this ritual anyway. You can repeat it on next month's full moon.

WHAT TO DO

1. Gather the following tools: a bowl of water, a bowl of flower petals of your choice, a bell (or anything that makes a ringing sound), salt, and three white candles.

2. In front of your self-worship Altar or space or just in a quiet place, set up the three candles side by side with some distance between them.

3. Place the bowl of water in front of you toward the left and the bowl of petals in front of you toward the right.

4. Light the candles, and ring the bell three times to cleanse the space. (OMG, bestie! As I wrote this sentence, someone on a bicycle nearby rang their bell! I had to share. #divinetiming)

5. Bring your hands into prayer position, close your eyes, take a deep breath, and make this sound: *aaaahhhhhh mmmmmmmmmm*. (The *ahh* is made with an open mouth, and the *mmm* is made with a closed mouth.) Repeat this seven times.

6. When you're ready, open your eyes and select one flower petal. Hold the petal up to your lips, whisper your desire/intention into it, and then gently blow on it and place it in the bowl of water. Repeat this process for each of your desires/intentions. (I suggest not doing more than five a month.)

7. When done, take a pinch of salt and sprinkle it into the bowl of water that now has the flower petals in it. The salt seals and protects your intentions.

8. Leave the bowl on your self-worship Altar for three sunrises. (For example, if you do the ritual today, start to count the sunrises tomorrow.)
9. At any time on the day of the third sunrise, take the bowl and pour it into a body of moving water (a river, the ocean, or even your toilet as it is flushing).

# Self-Reflection Journaling

What did you learn or gain from this experience today?

.............................................................................................................
.............................................................................................................
.............................................................................................................
.............................................................................................................
.............................................................................................................

Did you receive any downloads or experience any aha moments?

.............................................................................................................
.............................................................................................................
.............................................................................................................
.............................................................................................................
.............................................................................................................

Write three things you are proud of yourself for today.

.............................................................................................................
.............................................................................................................
.............................................................................................................
.............................................................................................................
.............................................................................................................

Write three things you are grateful for today.

.............................................................................................................
.............................................................................................................
.............................................................................................................
.............................................................................................................
.............................................................................................................

## Day 11: Cold-Shower Spell

Cold showers are super beneficial for you mentally, physically, and spiritually. They can increase endorphins, improve metabolism, support circulation, and help your body fight common illnesses. I personally love them for their spiritual benefits. They can reset you, open your crown, and give you an auric cleansing if done with the right intention, making for a magical AF shower experience.

### WHAT TO DO

First, you need to ease into the habit of taking cold showers. I know, hermana, at first I hated it, but I started to look forward to them after a few times. For the first shower, start by slowly lowering the temperature at the end of your regular shower, breathing deeply and centering your mind. Get the water cold enough that you feel uncomfortable. Then stay underneath it for two or three minutes. Repeat this process the next time you shower, but make the water slightly colder and go for another minute or two.

While you are under the cold water, follow this spell:

1. Allow yourself to be calm and be still. Tilt your head slightly back (be mindful not to go so far back that the water gets in your nose and mouth).
2. Start to focus on your womb (the area just above the vagina or groin). Create a little pressure in that region by activating the muscles there. Give it a good squeeze, like you are holding your pee, to help you identify the right muscles.
3. Once you start to feel tingling in your womb, lift it upward through your belly, through your chest, and out your mouth, feeling the energy like a wave within you. With practice, this can feel orgasmic; you are tapping into powerful feminine energy here.
4. At the same time, sweep your hands up your flesh, following the energy in your body from your womb, out of your mouth, and

continuing all the way up, with hands extended to the sky; then shake your hands once they are fully raised, as if you are shaking off the energy. (Breathe in as you place your hands on your womb and breathe out when you reach the top.)

5. These movements release blocks and wash out any negative energy lingering in the body, while filling your womb with rejuvenating, nourishing, and abundant energy. Abundant energy is great to work with for manifesting, spells, and rituals. And to work with it, all you have to do is simply tap into your womb, the source of all creation.

*Note:* If you're feeling sick or have recently been released from the hospital, please wait to do this spell until you are feeling better. If you are immunocompromised, please check with your doctor first.

# Self-Reflection Journaling

What did you learn or gain from this experience today?

..........................................................................................
..........................................................................................
..........................................................................................
..........................................................................................
..........................................................................................

Did you receive any downloads or experience any aha moments?

..........................................................................................
..........................................................................................
..........................................................................................
..........................................................................................
..........................................................................................

Write three things you are proud of yourself for today.

..........................................................................................
..........................................................................................
..........................................................................................
..........................................................................................
..........................................................................................

Write three things you are grateful for today.

..........................................................................................
..........................................................................................
..........................................................................................
..........................................................................................
..........................................................................................

## *Day 12: Intuitive Art Channeling*

Intuitive art channeling takes practice, but it is worth it! It taps deep into your intuition and channels messages, answers, and wisdom from your Divine Self. In this practice, you are tapping into only yourself—nothing outside of you. This is a way of using yourself as a divination tool. All you need is yourself, a crystal or objects representing the elements, and some crayons and paper.

Here are some ideas for crystals and objects that represent the elements:

- Earth: petrified wood, bronzite, yellow jasper, or copper; dirt, a plant, a branch, a rock, or a stone
- Air: selenite, pink calcite, amethyst, or white quartz; a feather, smoke, or incense
- Fire: carnelian, sunstone, or red jasper; a candle
- Water: amazonite or fluorite; a cup or bowl of water
- Spirit: You!

WHAT TO DO

Create a circle with the crystals and objects representing the elements; it should be big enough for you to fit in the center. Placing the Earth crystal or object directly in front of you, the air crystal or object to the left of you, the fire crystal or object at the back, and the water crystal or object toward the right. You are Spirit, in the center.

Get into a relaxed sitting position. Place the paper on the floor in front of you, and set the crayons beside the paper toward the right. Keep a few pieces of paper to the left of the paper in the center.

Take a deep breath, place your hands on your thighs, close your eyes, and start to sway gently from left to right. Start to connect your breaths with each sway. For example, when you sway to the right, breathe in, and exhale as you move to the left.

While swaying and breathing rhythmically, say in your mind, "In I go, inward to Divinity." Repeat this seven to eight times, or until you feel your body taking over and swaying where it wants; your head may start to gently roll as the energy begins to move through your body.

Then ask a question or simply say, "Bring forth your message for me today." Allow your non-dominant arm to reach for a crayon (keeping your eyes closed the entire time), and let your hand draw on the paper. Try not to force any movements or shapes. Let it happen naturally. With practice, the images, symbols, words, figures, and shapes become clearer.

If you feel like using more paper, reach for the paper to the left. Sometimes the message is laid out on different papers, and you have to put them together like a puzzle to reveal the bigger picture.

When you feel the rush leave, drop the crayon and come back to center, calm your body, and take a few slow deep breaths. Put your hands to your chest and say thank you to your Divine Self.

*Note:* You can reuse the crystals and objects; just cleanse and clear them before using them again.

# Self-Reflection Journaling

What did you learn or gain from this experience today?

........................................................................................................
........................................................................................................
........................................................................................................
........................................................................................................
........................................................................................................

Did you receive any downloads or experience any aha moments?

........................................................................................................
........................................................................................................
........................................................................................................
........................................................................................................
........................................................................................................

Write three things you are proud of yourself for today.

........................................................................................................
........................................................................................................
........................................................................................................
........................................................................................................
........................................................................................................

Write three things you are grateful for today.

........................................................................................................
........................................................................................................
........................................................................................................
........................................................................................................
........................................................................................................

## Day 13: Organize Your Finances

Yep, I went there. How do you expect to live your Divined life without looking at your money, bestie? Do you even know what your credit score is? I highly suggest you look into it and get a copy of the report. On that report, you can see who you owe and why your score is what it is. On YouTube or social media, there are many free videos that teach people how to read and understand credit reports and how to raise credit scores. There are also videos on investing. Yes, you can invest even if you don't make a lot of money. Small steps create bigger ones.

An important part of keeping your finances in good shape is getting yourself out of debt. But buying the things you want and going to the places you desire also involves organizing your finances. If I didn't organize mine, I would not have been able to purchase my forever home. It is never too early or too late to manifest your dreams! In fact, I just bought my first home two weeks ago! And I'm forty, and my hubby is forty-six. #go1stgeneration!

Don't worry, BFF; it may sound daunting, but it isn't as difficult as it seems. This may take a few days to do, but here are a few steps to guide you.


WHAT TO DO

Set up a filing system that works for you. It can be a box or files where you keep your receipts and bills, or you can file things electronically on your computer. The key is to keep all of your paperwork together in a safe place. Gather all of your bills, including your credit cards, utilities, phone, car payments, and so on. Organize them in whatever way works for you—you might use folders, spreadsheets, or computer software, to name a few ideas.

Creating a budget is a critical step in getting your finances in order, and it's a skill you can learn with the help of a budget calculator. Write down all your income sources, and then write down your monthly expenses, including your bills and debt. This is an excellent time to look at any monthly subscriptions and to see where you can cut back, especially if you are not using them. Tracking your spending is a helpful way to recognize what you are spending each month, which helps you stay within your budget. (When I did this step, I had to review my monthly bank statements and go into my phone's app store and PayPal to see if I was missing anything.)

Set up automatic bill payments and reminders. (This was the best thing I did for myself.) Once you know what bills you have to pay, you'll be in a better position to stay on top of your payments.

Balance payments with your paydays. Most people don't know that they can contact their credit card companies, utilities, and lenders to change monthly billing days to spread payments out over the month and not have them all come out of one week's paycheck.

Make a plan to tackle your debt. Evaluate how much you owe and how much you are paying in interest. There are free financial calculators that can help you determine how much you're paying; you can also call and find out directly from the source. Then find out how long it'll take for you to pay off your debts if you only make the minimum payments. I suggest talking to someone who helps organize finances about the best amount to pay so you can save money in the long run (check the QR code for sources). Once you have this information, you can set up a plan to chip away at your debt. Do what works best for you, but don't ignore it. Keep track, and have control over your debt.

Saving money gives us peace of mind and ensures that we'll have something to fall back on. If it hadn't been for my savings, 2020 would have been extremely hard for my family. I know way too many people who struggled due to COVID, people who got sick, lost their jobs, and didn't have backup plans. I tried to help as many families as I could, even people who I only knew because they followed my social media. It really opened my eyes to how vital savings are, and I am not blind to having the privilege to be able to save; for most of my life I didn't have much of anything, and even then, I tried my best to save money. I went from being homeless to being able to rent a room, to renting a small basement, to renting an apartment with a roommate, to renting on my own, and now I have my own house. It was a long process but one that was worth it. I know it can be hard. I did not grow up in a privileged home, and this is why helping you with this and everything in this book means so much #poquitoapoco. You got this, Bestie!

# Self-Reflection Journaling

What did you learn or gain from this experience today?

........................................................................................................
........................................................................................................
........................................................................................................
........................................................................................................
........................................................................................................

Did you receive any downloads or experience any aha moments?

........................................................................................................
........................................................................................................
........................................................................................................
........................................................................................................
........................................................................................................

Write three things you are proud of yourself for today.

........................................................................................................
........................................................................................................
........................................................................................................
........................................................................................................
........................................................................................................

Write three things you are grateful for today.

........................................................................................................
........................................................................................................
........................................................................................................
........................................................................................................
........................................................................................................

## *Day 14: Love Your Life*

Make a list of the colors and style of clothing you wear, the music you listen to, the foods you eat, the places you like to go, and the self-care and beauty products you buy.

Then scan each one and ask yourself the following questions:

"Am I aligned with these things, or am I influenced by something other than self?"

"What do I really like to shop for, listen to, eat, visit, and buy?"

"Where do I really want to go or start going?"

"Are these products supporting me, working for me, and aligned with what I feel I need?"

"Is there a better way for me to be spending my money that is more in alignment with my values and who I am?"

# Self-Reflection Journaling

What did you learn or gain from this experience today?

........................................................................................

........................................................................................

........................................................................................

........................................................................................

........................................................................................

Did you receive any downloads or experience any aha moments?

........................................................................................

........................................................................................

........................................................................................

........................................................................................

........................................................................................

Write three things you are proud of yourself for today.

........................................................................................

........................................................................................

........................................................................................

........................................................................................

........................................................................................

Write three things you are grateful for today.

........................................................................................

........................................................................................

........................................................................................

........................................................................................

........................................................................................

## Day 15: Overcoming the Urge

Overcoming the urge to do things you have grown used to or addicted to is fucking hard, BFF. In this instance, we are talking about social media. By now, you should know I am a big fan of unplugging from my devices to plug better into self. It is essential to practice self-patience and learn how to overcome the urges.

### WHAT TO DO

Stay off social media today and stay away from your devices. Every time you feel the urge or even think about it, direct your mind to your breath and center yourself. You can do this by taking three deep breaths and then gently patting on your heart center while saying, "I am in control of my decisions, I am in charge of my actions, I can do this."

# Self-Reflection Journaling

What did you learn or gain from this experience today?

.............................................................................................................

.............................................................................................................

.............................................................................................................

.............................................................................................................

.............................................................................................................

Did you receive any downloads or experience any aha moments?

.............................................................................................................

.............................................................................................................

.............................................................................................................

.............................................................................................................

.............................................................................................................

Write three things you are proud of yourself for today.

.............................................................................................................

.............................................................................................................

.............................................................................................................

.............................................................................................................

.............................................................................................................

Write three things you are grateful for today.

.............................................................................................................

.............................................................................................................

.............................................................................................................

.............................................................................................................

.............................................................................................................

## *Day 16: Shake It Up*

Reach out to a friend or someone in your community and spend the day with them. Don't plan anything, and don't have any expectations. Just ask if they are willing to spend some time with you, and allow your Spirits to connect. Be spontaneous.

Sometimes, I grab my mother and I say, "Vamos a perdernos." *Let's get lost.* We allow ourselves to just take it moment by moment and drive around while conversing. Usually, these are the most healing conversations we have with each other. If we stop at a place, we check it out. If we feel like eating a certain food, we find it. It is all about just being present and gifting yourself a day of unexpected adventure.

# Self-Reflection Journaling

What did you learn or gain from this experience today?

.............................................................................................
.............................................................................................
.............................................................................................
.............................................................................................
.............................................................................................

Did you receive any downloads or experience any aha moments?

.............................................................................................
.............................................................................................
.............................................................................................
.............................................................................................
.............................................................................................

Write three things you are proud of yourself for today.

.............................................................................................
.............................................................................................
.............................................................................................
.............................................................................................
.............................................................................................

Write three things you are grateful for today.

.............................................................................................
.............................................................................................
.............................................................................................
.............................................................................................
.............................................................................................

## Day 17: A Life Vision Box

Instead of a board, I love to use a box for my life vision. When I was a kid, a teacher of mine brought in a pretty box with glitter on it, filled with poems and pictures of other countries—it even had affirmations on the outside of it. I politely asked her what the box was for, and she said it contained her bucket list. "A bucket list?" I asked. "Yes," she replied, "a bucket list is all the things you want to do, see, and experience before you leave this Earth." It inspired me to do the same, but with a little twist. I created a life vision box.

### WHAT TO DO

First, get yourself a box. It can be a fancy box or a simple one. I used a shoebox for many years.

Add your flair to it, and add a magical touch by embedding it with your intention. You can paint on it, draw on it or in it, or add pictures or words—whatever you like.

Then start to put items in the box that represent things you want to manifest or accomplish, places you want to visit, or things you want to experience. Use your imagination; the possibilities are endless. You hold the power to manifest them.

Keep your box to yourself; do not share it with anyone else. It is secret. If you are living with your family or a partner and they find it, no worries. It won't do anything to your box. The point is to try and keep your dreams and aspirations to yourself. You don't want anyone else's energy or bad juju fucking with your vision vibes.

Continue to add to your vision box through the years, and make sure to go through it every spring, cleaning out what you already manifested and adding new visions.

# Self-Reflection Journaling

What did you learn or gain from this experience today?

........................................................................................
........................................................................................
........................................................................................
........................................................................................
........................................................................................

Did you receive any downloads or experience any aha moments?

........................................................................................
........................................................................................
........................................................................................
........................................................................................
........................................................................................

Write three things you are proud of yourself for today.

........................................................................................
........................................................................................
........................................................................................
........................................................................................
........................................................................................

Write three things you are grateful for today.

........................................................................................
........................................................................................
........................................................................................
........................................................................................
........................................................................................

## Day 18: New-Self Introduction

The new-self introduction is your way of saying to the world, *Here I am as I am, bitches!* Okay, okay, I get overly excited sometimes, but I am so excited for you!

### WHAT TO DO

Prepare what you want to say, and plan how you will reach your audience. You can do a post or video on social media, FaceTime with your friends, and or have a meeting with your family via Zoom. Any way you want to do it is fine—there is no right or wrong way.

The goal is to introduce the new you and make it clear that this is who you are. Many people will stay stuck on who you used to be, especially family members who swear they know you best but are sometimes the ones who don't get you at all. Remember, it is not your responsibility to change their minds. Do you, be you, and keep moving! Pa'lante!

# Self-Reflection Journaling

What did you learn or gain from this experience today?

.................................................................................................
.................................................................................................
.................................................................................................
.................................................................................................
.................................................................................................

Did you receive any downloads or experience any aha moments?

.................................................................................................
.................................................................................................
.................................................................................................
.................................................................................................
.................................................................................................

Write three things you are proud of yourself for today.

.................................................................................................
.................................................................................................
.................................................................................................
.................................................................................................
.................................................................................................

Write three things you are grateful for today.

.................................................................................................
.................................................................................................
.................................................................................................
.................................................................................................
.................................................................................................

## Day 19: Tea Ritual for Presence

This tea ritual for presence will help you come back to center and find yourself right where you are. It is a daily ritual in my home. Coming back to self is my number one priority, and this ritual has been a powerful addition to my evening routine. You can do this practice at any time of day. It should feel like you are stepping into another realm, a refuge of sacredness and serenity.

WHAT TO DO

Plan for a thirty- to sixty-minute break, in a space where you can be comfortable and remain undisturbed.

Decide what you will be doing during this break, such as simply sipping, journaling, reading, etc.

While the tea is brewing, stand with your feet hip-width apart (I suggest barefoot), and cross your arms over your chest (like a vampire, hehe). Keep your eyes gently closed and take slow deep breaths.

Once the tea is ready, head to your space and get comfy.

Practice mindfulness with your tea ritual to help you come back into your body and into the present moment.

Gaze at the tea and notice how it looks and moves.

Place it close enough to yourself that you are able to take in its aromas. Inhale the scent of the tea through your nose and then slowly exhale.

Feel the warmth of the cup in your hands, and appreciate its energy embracing you.

Take the first sip, and allow the flavors to swirl in your mouth for a few seconds as you slowly roll your tongue up and around the sacred liquid. When ready, swallow while sinking into a place of deep enjoyment and gratitude.

Open your awareness by softening your eyes, face, and heart. With this ritual, you are invited to relax into yourself and enjoy your presence as is. At this moment, the rest of the world does not exist.

# Self-Reflection Journaling

What did you learn or gain from this experience today?

..................................................................................................
..................................................................................................
..................................................................................................
..................................................................................................
..................................................................................................

Did you receive any downloads or experience any aha moments?

..................................................................................................
..................................................................................................
..................................................................................................
..................................................................................................
..................................................................................................

Write three things you are proud of yourself for today.

..................................................................................................
..................................................................................................
..................................................................................................
..................................................................................................
..................................................................................................

Write three things you are grateful for today.

..................................................................................................
..................................................................................................
..................................................................................................
..................................................................................................
..................................................................................................

## Day 20: Rewrite Your Story

In this exercise, you will write a short story that features yourself as the main character, but this story will be a little different from most. Most stories are based on action, but I want you to tell a story about rest and what it means to you. Share what it means for you to be still. Visualize what it looks and feels like to fully rest and take a break, slow down, and be present. What are you doing? Who do you become? What do you choose to eat and drink, what are you listening to, who is with you, are you alone?

Rest does not have to be sleep or a nap (though it is truly important to get enough sleep). Rest can mean having a chill day and putting on some vibing music of your choice. I had Nina Simone on replay and even started a Pandora station that plays songs similar to her vibes and music. Give it a try. Thank me later, bestie.

After you write this short story, live it. Go for it. You deserve to rest in the way that supports you best.

# Self-Reflection Journaling

What did you learn or gain from this experience today?

.................................................................................................
.................................................................................................
.................................................................................................
.................................................................................................
.................................................................................................

Did you receive any downloads or experience any aha moments?

.................................................................................................
.................................................................................................
.................................................................................................
.................................................................................................
.................................................................................................

Write three things you are proud of yourself for today.

.................................................................................................
.................................................................................................
.................................................................................................
.................................................................................................
.................................................................................................

Write three things you are grateful for today.

.................................................................................................
.................................................................................................
.................................................................................................
.................................................................................................
.................................................................................................

## Day 21: Meditation Ritual for Returning to Self and Releasing What No Longer Serves You

This is the meditation ritual I shared about in the beginning of this book, before I woke and was reborn. This meditation's intention is to help you come back home to self by releasing what no longer serves you and connecting you to your heart and Divine presence.

### WHAT TO DO

Find a quiet space where you can sit or lie comfortably. Once you're settled, close your eyes or soften your gaze and tune in to your breath. Notice your breath without trying to change it. Stay in this space for a moment.

Inhale through your nose and then exhale through your mouth. Continue to take slow, deep full breaths. Repeat seven to eight times.

As you breathe, become aware of the state of your body and the quality of your mind. Where is your body holding tension? What emotions are present? Where is your mind? Is it wandering, or is it at home within the breath?

Place both hands over your heart and continue to inhale through your nose and exhale through your mouth. Ask yourself: How does it feel to place my hands over this tender area, this place where I experience love for self and others?

Let your breath become smoother and more effortless. Feel the flow of air moving into your lungs and out of your body.

With each exhale, imagine you are releasing any negative thoughts or feelings, being mindful to let go of any uncomfortable feelings in your body, and flushing them out with every exhale as they evaporate into nothingness.

Continue to focus on your breath. On each inhale, think, "I am home," and on each exhale, think, "I release you." Let each inhale draw in love and each exhale release what is no longer serving you. Take a few minutes to breathe in and recite this mantra internally. Notice how you feel as you say these words to yourself.

If your mind wanders at any point, know that it's okay. It's the nature of the mind to wander. Simply bring your attention back to the breath. Now visualize yourself standing in front of a mirror and looking into your own eyes. What do you see? Pain and sadness? Love and joy? Neutrality?

Regardless of what appears in the reflection, tell yourself: "I am safe in myself," "I am here for you," and "I am home." Repeat each of these statements three times.

Imagine now that you can breathe into your heart, and visualize love pouring back out into your hands. Let this love permeate you from the heart center, filling the rest of your body.

Feel a sense of comfort and calm traveling up through your chest; into your neck and head; out into your shoulders, arms, and hands; and then down into your ribs, belly, pelvis, legs, and feet.

Allow a sensation of warmth to fill you from head to toe. Breathe here and know that love is always available when you need it. Take a moment to focus on this feeling and breath.

When you're ready, take a few more slow, deep, mindful breaths, and then softly open your eyes. Sit for a few moments to acknowledge the unique experience you had during this meditation.

This is a beautiful opportunity to learn something new about yourself and tune in to your physical and emotional needs. Let self-love help you build a stronger relationship with yourself and allow you to show up more fully in your life.

# Self-Reflection Journaling

What did you learn or gain from this experience today?

.................................................................................................................
.................................................................................................................
.................................................................................................................
.................................................................................................................
.................................................................................................................

Did you receive any downloads or ah-ha moments?

.................................................................................................................
.................................................................................................................
.................................................................................................................
.................................................................................................................
.................................................................................................................

Write three things you are proud of yourself for today.

.................................................................................................................
.................................................................................................................
.................................................................................................................
.................................................................................................................
.................................................................................................................

Write three things you are grateful for today.

.................................................................................................................
.................................................................................................................
.................................................................................................................
.................................................................................................................
.................................................................................................................

**DEVOTIONAL**

# Self-Activism through Community Care

Over the last few generations, community has been withering away from day-to-day lives. We have become accustomed to hibernating in our homes and dismissing the life-altering benefits of being with our communities. Online communities have been on the rise, and that's fantastic—I even have one, Spiritual Baddie Coven. However, you cannot virtually re-create real authentic physical community. You can't re-create the magic that happens in the presence of one another, the soul connections that occur when we're up close and personal. Because being in community is and always has been our collective way of supporting, loving, caring for, protecting, and amplifying one another.

I started the Brujx Movement in July of 2021, showing up through Ceremony and community, offering healing, song, dance, prayers, and unity in times of need. But the real birth of the movement started long before that. When I was a little girl, community was everything to me, and it is also one of the reasons I survived my childhood. My mother was not the only one who raised me; my community did as well.

Luz, a Puerto Rican spiritualist from the sixth floor of my building, was the one who taught me the difference between a human and different kinds of Spirits. She knew I was able to see Spirits and saw me conversing with them, not realizing that some of them were Spirits. She taught me that some Spirits were so strong in energy that they looked more human than the others. She wore white all the time, and she would put my hair up and cover it with a white head wrap to protect my Spirit. She would fill my pockets with caracoles (shells) to keep me from floating out of this realm. Before she passed, she told me something that will forever stay with me: "Somos como el Mar, femenino y masculino, guiado por el espíritu de la luna. Lobas, que prosperan por estar en una comunidad." *We are all like the Ocean. Both feminine and masculine, led by the Spirit of the moon. We are wolves, who thrive from being in community.*

She was my spiritual mother, the one who also gave me weekly Limpias and checked in on my energy to help me remove traumatic emotions and experiences from my body. This was her way of showing up for me, and it was how she showed up for many others.

Armando was an old Cuban man who was nearly in his eighties and ran a bodega across the street from the building where I lived. My own grandparents were in Cuba and I had never met them in person, so he was the grandfather I never had. I would spend a lot of time in his bodega; he would even call me his brujita Cubana. I remember the first day I met him, he was tending to a single mother who was crying because she did not have enough money to buy milk or diapers for her babies. I remember having this sinking feeling in my stomach; I felt her pain and worry like it was my own. My Spirit connected to her Spirit, and I felt her as if I were her. This is what community does. You aren't able to swipe away real human emotions, experiences, and hardships. Instead, they remind you of the need for human connection and the importance of humanity and community care.

That day in Armando's bodega, I started to cry and shake but was immediately calmed by what happened next. Armando gave her fiao, meaning "take what you need now and pay me later." It's a trust system of credit where the shopkeeper takes a chance that you, the customer, will honor his trust and pay him back. My heart was blown. What did I just witness? I was too young to fully understand, but I can tell you that what he did felt like love. Armando offered fiao to lots of people, including my own mother, teaching me that to be part of community, you have to truly *be a part* of it. With this selfless gesture, he was building not only a loyal customer base but also a community whose members counted on one another.

Community care is activism, it isn't just about protesting, marching, rallying, or working for things like better infrastructure in low-income communities. These are all extremely important, but community care can be a much quieter act because it is also about our interpersonal social networks. Many people can't self-care on their own or don't have the means to be able to. This is why community care in the form of showing up for others is vital not only for their survival and well-being but also for keeping ourselves activated in Spirit, which offers us a whole new way to heal as well.

In 2020, I needed community care. I needed my friends, family, and neighbors to show up for me. I was never one to ask for help or admit when I was struggling, but that year, I learned how to. Because of the care I received, I was able to come out of a deep depression and come home to self. The love and care that people gave to me in person was priceless, and that should be how we function as a community. I've had friends who at times were so physically and mentally exhausted that they were unable to clean their homes, do their laundry, cook food for themselves, or even bathe. And the right thing to do is to show up—not to just call or text, but to appear at someone's doorstep because sometimes that's just what people need. They need for someone to truly show up. Just like Armando and Luz.

So how can we build a community that is loyal, one that not only gives but also receives with open hearts? We start by showing up. We go to our friends, and we ask how we can help. We clean for them, do their laundry, cook them a meal, or bring takeout. I've bathed my friends before, set their baths and literally washed them from head to toe. This is love, this is community care, this is activism. We learn not only how to hold space for one another but also how to hold one another.

*Self-care is essential, yes, but community care is also essential*
*for your well-being and your connection to the Divine Self.*

How is community care an essential form of activism? Capitalist society and culture have programmed us to be ashamed of our struggles, hardships, and need for help. The wellness industry is constantly telling you how to care for yourself, without mentioning that asking someone else for help is also okay and nothing to be ashamed of. We need to learn that we are not burdens and that our need for care is just as human as our ability to offer care to one another.

Community care can look like many things, from watching your neighbor's child while she takes time to rest or grabbing groceries for your elders in the community. It all comes back to just showing up for one another.

You can't capitalize or monetize community care as the wellness industry does for self-care. Working outside of the system is anti-capitalism, which makes community care a vital and powerful form of activism. My hope is that you think about this, asking yourself if community care is something you want to be part of. Start with friends; ask how you can support them. Or reach out to your neighbors and introduce yourself, start creating friendships, and open up conversations about how you can be there for one another. Growing up, I remember when a knock on the door usually meant someone was there to ask for a cup of sugar or milk. These are beautiful acts, ones which today can be far too rare.

Think about how you may already be doing community care right now. For example, my husband, Will, is already doing a form of it. There's an elderly man where we used to live who finds comfort in conversing with Will. So sometimes Will goes to his house and simply has a beer and a chat with him, and often he gardens with him as well. The elder trusts Will, and so he sometimes asks him to help with small things around the house. These are all small gestures, but they can have huge impacts in people's lives.

---

## The Community Care Challenge

Like with any form of activism, we can't expect change overnight. Community care can't be performative. Building community takes practice, effort, and commitment, and it requires that we get out of our comfort zones and get comfortable showing up for one another. Ultimately, community care leads us back to ourselves.

Self-activism is about honoring the Divine by standing up for ourselves and one another. As you move through the following challenges, think about how you can make them consistent efforts in your life and how you can elevate them from being routines into becoming rituals.

1. What is one thing you could do this week to improve your local community? How would you accomplish this goal? And why is it important to you and the people who live there?

2. Spend one week doing something kind for someone else every single day. It doesn't have to be a grand gesture; it can be as easy as painting a door for your elderly neighbors that haven't been able to do it themselves or running an errand for a friend. At the end of the week, write about what you did and how it impacted the people you helped. Then explain what you learned about yourself during this week.

3. I want you to dream for a moment. If you could start your own charity or nonprofit, what would its mission be, and who would it serve? How could you start helping that same community today?

4. Be vulnerable on this one and be honest: What kind of community care do you need? Without feeling shame or like you should be able to do these things yourself, identify where could you use assistance.

5. Gather your besties and have a day of brainstorming together. Walk around your community—or, if you are privileged, walk around a marginalized community—and see for yourselves how you might be able to offer community care. (If you do this in a community that is not yours, please remember to be respectful. You do not know what problems these community members might have, and likely you won't be sure of the answers. Talk to local people and shop owners about their concerns, and ask them how you and your friends can help.)

# Liberation Is Living in Alignment with Our Ancestors

Self-activism is checking in on yourself and prioritizing yourself while also showing up for your community—but not just the people around you. Your community also includes the people that came before you. Remember that our ancestors want for us what they never had. Self-activism is the recognition that we can be their dream realized. But we can't realize their dreams alone. You should never feel shame for needing support from community. The belief that you should feel shame needs to be eradicated. When we disrupt these assumptions, we can begin to reprogram the whole system. Our self-care and our community care are interconnected. We want for others what we want for ourselves.

In my own experience with self-activism, I've learned to be more vulnerable with myself and to allow myself to acknowledge where I need more support. There is power in asking for help, even when your ego tells you it's weak. We discover our deepest truths when we are in alignment with the Divine, and Divinity lives in all. That is why none of us will ever truly be free until all of us are free.

My ancestors endured too much for me to be living a life that isn't in line with my truth. They would want me to have a life steeped in honor and reverence, a life that isn't run by colonialist, racist, capitalist systems and societies. They would want me to dismantle this world that has built barriers between myself and humanity, so that I am reminded that my story and my life are more than just sorrows. They would want me to have patience in my healing, growth, and transformation; it is a lifelong journey. But also, they would want me to be grateful that I am able to receive the healing, growth, and transformation that was denied to them.

Self-activism is my way of saying, "You can never erase my ancestors from within my Spirit." Self-activism is my way of fighting spiritual oppression by connecting to my roots, my Divine Self, and my people in the name of living my Divined life. I found myself through self-activism when the world was squeezing me into a box that could not sustain me. In fact, I was being suffocated by it.

Ultimately, self-worship, discovery, and activism all work together to liberate the self in much the same way that we declutter our homes. We remove the things that just don't align with us anymore only to discover the parts of ourselves that bring true joy, that have real value. We are able to see the Divined life that our ancestors died for, the one we are responsible for creating.

When we begin to see everything for what it is, we are able to transcend and heal from the lies of a system built and maintained to enslave us—economically, physically, mentally, sexually, spiritually. Liberation means freedom. *Libertad!!* Our purpose is not just to save ourselves; when we participate in collective liberations, we save the world. We liberate our Divine Self from the entrapment and enslavement of those who place profit before people, before Spirit, before life.

My people are literally dying right now in Cuba, bleeding for their liberation on the streets, fighting in community with one another for the right of living a life they deserve and want, one that is free from the oppression of dictatorship, one that supports their basic human rights and needs. And over here, we're focused on bubble baths and cotton candy aesthetics, all while feeding the very same oppressors who are murdering us, hurting us, and dimming our Spirits. Our people need for us to show up for ourselves so that we can better show up for them.

The world needs us to know who we are so deeply that we are better able to manifest a new world together, a Divine life that doesn't sell you water from the very Earth from which we were all born.

When we are liberated in Spirit, we attune to this Divine life, one which shares space with and wholly supports not only your Divine Spirit and human experience but also community care. Through this activism, we disrupt those same systems that are responsible for our intergenerational trauma, that forced our ancestors into lives and beliefs that weren't their own. Those same systems are still trying to erase who we are, but when we liberate ourselves and heal these ancestral traumas, we heal the ancestors as well, cutting off the chains and demanding what was taken from them, demanding what we all deserve. At the root of who we are, we all want a life that is safe and equitable and unified for ourselves, our children, and our families. The Divine Self is asking that we do more than take bubble baths and create vision boards (though obviously I love those too, bestie). No, friend, this is where shit gets real. Magic and manifestation are only authentic powers when they are infused with justice, when they are powered by our liberation.

I will not silence my story, I will no longer play small, and neither should you. We are only truly fully free when we are all free. To live our Divined lives, we must be willing to stand up and break the cage. Together we will rise; together we will wake.

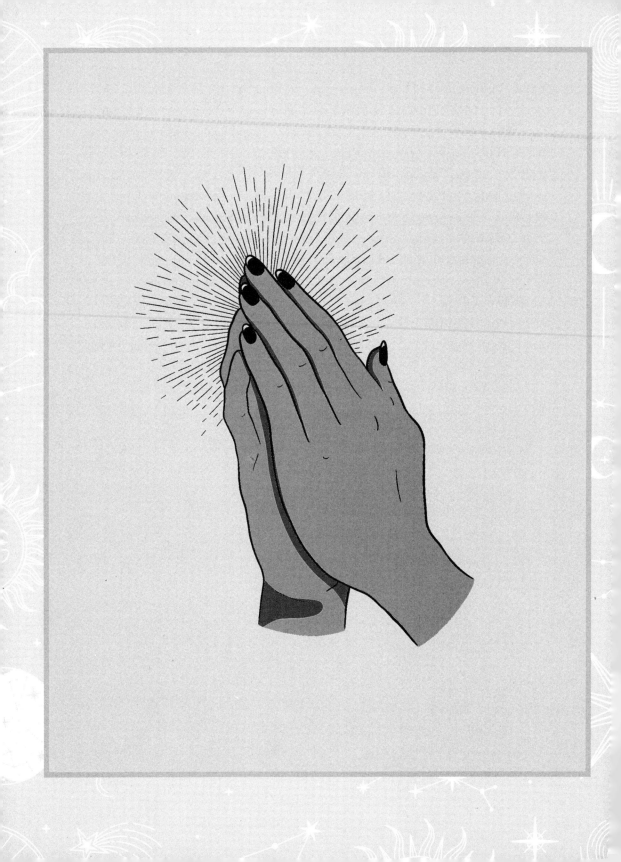

# Sacred Truths

Self-activism is you activated in truth, but to get to this place, we must work to decolonize spirituality, which has stripped us of our innate powers and liberation. We must overcome the inner critic and external systems that keep us from seeing the best in ourselves, while developing fundamental and essential strengths in self, compassion, mindfulness, and self-acceptance. When we learn to build a solid and trustworthy relationship with the Divine Self, we begin to liberate all parts of ourselves—economically, physically, mentally, sexually, and spiritually.

When the world tells you that you aren't good enough, worthy, or capable, your self-activism shuts that shit down. When the world tells you what your life should look and feel like, what jobs or ways of making money are worthy of a successful life, self-activism cuts those cords from your Spirit. When the world is pushing hustle culture and your self-care is deemed a luxury, self-activism disrupts those violent beliefs and opens your eyes to what self-care can be, something that is accessible to all and not just to the privileged.

Self-activism is learning to become the ritual in life's Ceremony. Yes, we can create a life that manifests more joy and peace, one that supports us wholly and intentionally. We learn to be gentle with ourselves through self-love and self-care. But we also learn that self-activism is the root of activism. Once we put on the oxygen mask for ourselves, we must turn to our communities; we must show up. There is no manifestation without humanity. That is only greed. True manifestation is about wanting and demanding liberation for the world, so that we can all live in Divinity, healed by the power of human magic and connected to each other through dark oceans and the stillness of the galaxies within.

# Self-Activism Prompts

1. In our day-to-day lives, we put up with what we have become used to and often don't stop to consider that we can change aspects of our daily lives to better support ourselves rather than cause harm.

   PROMPT: What parts of daily life cause you stress, anxiety, frustration, worry, fear, or sadness? What can you do to change those experiences?

2. Everyone seems to be selling something new every day, from the best way to eat to the best workouts, beauty products, and so on. It can be overwhelming and can honestly leave you feeling lost and unsure of what is best for you. They sell us brokenness with the lie of perfection.

   PROMPT: You are the only one that has been with you since the day you took your first breath. Make a list of what you feel is vital to your mental, physical, emotional, and spiritual well-being to give you a foundation for knowing your priorities. (For example: eating cleaner, moving your body, healing your heart, supporting your mental health, etc.) Explain in detail why the things on your list are important to you and what you can do to grow in these areas.

3. We need to start normalizing asking for help.

> PROMPT: If you had the chance to change something in your life, what would it be? Think about things that directly affect or impact you and your well-being. And then ask yourself, "What can I do about this?" Is it something you can do yourself, or do you need the support of others? Your community?

..............................................................................................
..............................................................................................
..............................................................................................
..............................................................................................
..............................................................................................

4. We want to try to do a multitude of things for ourselves and our communities, but we often push them aside and never get to them. I'm a death doula and have come across many souls who, at their death beds, wished they could have done more of what brought them joy.

> PROMPT: Make a list of the things that bring meaning into your life. Are they people, places, moments, or things? If you can't think of any, ask yourself if you've ever had any. What can you find in your life right now that gives it meaning? What can you do to find meaning in your life?

..............................................................................................
..............................................................................................
..............................................................................................
..............................................................................................
..............................................................................................

5. Allow yourself to be completely vulnerable and let truth lead you in this question. Too often, we think we have to do it all—run the business, manage the kids, do the laundry, pick up the groceries, ay! The list goes on. But there are ways to ask others to care for us. In fact, community care is one of the most powerful forms of self-activism when we are the ones to receive it.

PROMPT: How do you believe community can show up for you? How can you stop resisting your own needs and begin to ask for support? What would being supported feel like?

.............................................................................................................
.............................................................................................................
.............................................................................................................
.............................................................................................................
.............................................................................................................

6. Community care is critical for self-activism. Through being in community with others, we are able to heal not only ourselves but also the world.

PROMPT: How do you think you can show up for others in your community? What acts of support can you offer? And how do you plan on implementing these acts as a form of community care?

.............................................................................................................
.............................................................................................................
.............................................................................................................
.............................................................................................................
.............................................................................................................

7. Dream big, bestie! You deserve and are worthy of the world that you desire. Creating a clear vision of what that world is and why you want it is vital in manifesting it.

PROMPT: What would your life look and feel like if you were given a magic wand to make it happen? Be as detailed as possible, and stick to your values and authentic needs and wants. Then ask yourself, Can this be something I work toward? How? Write a letter to yourself. In this letter, tell yourself your plans moving forward with your mind, body, soul, and life. This should be a promise of sorts that you will try your best to keep.

.............................................................................................................
.............................................................................................................

.............................................................................................................
.....................................................     ...............................................................
.............................................................................................................

**8.** Life can seem mundane when we are busy, not present, and not allowing ourselves to experience life outside of the same old routines. Where's the magic?

> **PROMPT:** O magic, magic, wherefore art thou, magic? It is *everywhere*! It is within and without, waiting for you to notice it, play with it, and dwell in it. Write about the times you felt or saw magic in your life. When we acknowledge magic being present, it becomes our reality. You will start to see it in the winds, the trees, the lands, and the waters. Magic will greet you through animals, people, the seasons, and the stars shining above you. But most importantly, remember that the magic is within you.

.............................................................................................................
.............................................................................................................
.............................................................................................................
.............................................................................................................
.............................................................................................................

# A Love Letter

Dear Best Friend,

Although we have come to the end of this book, it does not represent the end of our friendship or your journey. I hope that this book awakened something in you and brought you closer to your truth and who you truly are. I hope that it gave you peace of mind and confidence in journeying fully present and trusting in your Divine Self—liberating you from societal chains and harmful spiritual narratives.

I want to remind you that you are powerful and have an army of ancestors, Spirits, and guides surrounding you with their embrace and cheering you on. Continue with your practice, continue unveiling yourself, and shine as brightly as you can.

You are not here to become; you already are.

You came through the portal of the sacred womb as a healer, Divine, sacred, and magical AF.

You are a born storyteller; raise your voice and allow the ancestors to speak revolutions through you.

You are rooted in the songs of medicine flowing through the Earth and the celestial melodies humming in the skies.

Your intuition is full of wisdom and lifetimes of experience, guiding and protecting you.

Don't allow anything or anyone to separate you from this truth, for by doing so, they are breaking the union that is meant to be with us all. United, together, we reclaim our collective power and remembrance.

Remember that each one of us has the power to influence and teach one another and the younger generations that come after us. Through embracing our truths, we help awaken those around us and pass down the light that keeps our worlds illuminated.

I believe there is such a thing as evil and that it hides in plain sight, trying to separate us from ourselves and each other, dividing us by making us hate ourselves and each other. However, I also believe that we are armed with the tools to overcome this evil and reveal its face(s).

You are not small or insignificant. You are mighty and carry strength, resilience, and power in your bones. You are born with ancient spells, medicine, and wisdom in your blood.

Before Earth, you came from the stars. You will go back to the stars soon enough, dear friend, but for now, your journey on Earth calls for your presence and embodied human experience. You may feel like you're alone, lost, or not really home, but the stars gave you a piece of home within. You are home because you are the stars. You are the Earth. Come back home to self, dear friend, and all will be revealed.

Please remember, you don't always have to be *on* to make progress. You don't always need to be in a positive mood or state to manifest. You don't have to do things the way others do them to realize your truth and live your Divined life.

It should be your priority to make time for yourself and create more joy in your life because, bestie, you are worthy. Never take things too seriously. Know that you are always protected and Divinely loved. You are the only one in control of your life, and, most importantly, you are now living a life led by Spirit.

You are a living Altar, and all you need is within you. #thealtarwithin

Love,

Juliet

# Acknowledgments

I would like to thank my husband. He is my rock, never questioning the paths on which Spirit takes me and always there to walk alongside me no matter what the journey entails. He is my protector, my Lobo (wolf).

Thank you to my children, Myka and Aidan, for being the very best souls any mama could ask for. You have been patient and understanding, never once complaining when mommy has to get to writing her books. Instead, you are always super supportive and give me tons of love and hugs each day, which has helped me stay focused on my mission to make this a better and safer world for us all.

To Row House, I once said that you are a breath of fresh air, but after writing this book, I now realize that You. Are. Breath. You're a breath I had not been able to take before, due to being silenced, whitewashed, edited until I was digestible, and boxed into what the publishing world thought I should be and should sound like—a world run by capitalist, racist systems and programs that use authors to make quotas but that don't really give a fuck about what we are saying.

You are a breath that has filled this book with power, giving it life and truth because it is real, authentic, and raw. Thank you for breathing for those of us who were suffocating. We will breathe together until all the voices that have been silenced are heard.

# About the Author

Juliet Diaz is a Bruja, Seer, and Spiritual activist. She's an Indigenous Taino Cubana from a long line of curanderos (Healers) and Brujas on both sides of her parents' lineages. She believes Magic lives within us all and feels passionately about inspiring others to step into their truth and wake to their remembrance. Juliet has devoted her life to helping people come back to their Divine Self and liberate themselves from the oppressor within and without. She's the creator of Spiritual Baddie Coven, her brand and online membership community.

Juliet has a Master of Science in Herbal Medicine and countless certifications in an array of healing modalities. She has been featured in major publications like *Oprah Magazine*, *National Geographic*, the *Atlantic*, *Wired*, and Refinery29, to name a few.

She is the author of the bestselling book *Witchery: Embrace the Witch Within* (which has sold to over nine countries) and the #1 new release *Plant Witchery*. *The Altar Within* is her third and most important book yet.

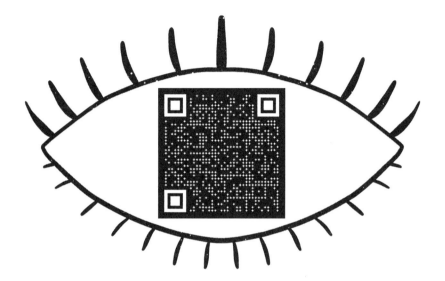